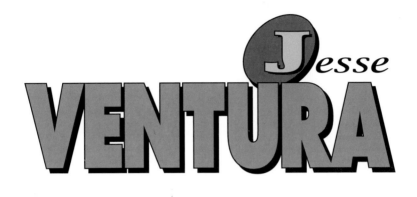

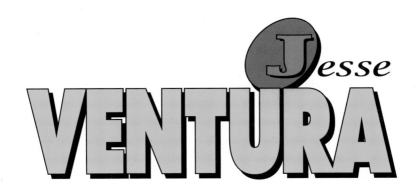

Biography®

Jesse VENTURA

Keith Elliot Greenberg

Lerner Publications Company
Minneapolis

This book is an unauthorized biography and is not sponsored, authorized, or endorsed by or affiliated with Jesse Ventura or his family. Any compensation for the use of photographic images was donated to Ventura for Minnesota, Incorporated.

This book is available in two bindings:
Library binding by Lerner Publications Company
Softcover by First Avenue Editions
Divisions of Lerner Publishing Group
241 First Avenue North
Minneapolis, MN 55401 U.S.A.

Website address: www.lernerbooks.com

Library of Congress Cataloging-in-Publication Data

Greenberg, Keith Elliot.
   Jesse Ventura / by Keith Greenberg.
     p.   cm. — (A&E biography)
   Includes bibliographical references and index.
   Summary: A biography of the former professional wrestler and radio talk show host who in 1998 became the governor of Minnesota.
   ISBN 0-8225-4977-8 (alk. paper). — ISBN 0-8225-9680-6 (pbk. : alk. paper) 1. Ventura, Jesse Juvenile literature. 2. Governors—Minnesota Biography Juvenile literature. 3. Minnesota—Politics and government—1951—Juvenile literature. [1. Ventura, Jesse.
2. Governors.] I. Title. II. Series.
   F610.G74 2000
   677.6'053'092—dc21
   [B]   99-13281

Manufactured in the United States of America
1 2 3 4 5 6 – JR – 05 04 03 02 01 00

CONTENTS

Jesse takes the oath of office with his family by his side. From middle left to right: **wife Terry, daughter Jade, and son Tyrel.**

Chapter **ONE**

SHOCKING THE WORLD

THE WIND HOWLED DOWN THE FRONT STEPS OF THE Minnesota State Capitol, toward the television trucks parked across a field of white snow. The temperature was twelve degrees below zero, but the chilly air actually felt thirty degrees colder. Still, the curious crowds could not stay away. Wearing heavy parkas and wool hats, with scarves wrapped around their faces, reporters from as far away as Japan huddled under the frosty sky. Meanwhile, more than six hundred citizens were arriving at the Capitol building. They worked on farms and in factories, offices, and department stores. There were college students, mothers with babies, businesspeople in suits, and elderly people with white hair and stories about World War II and the Great

Depression. What united these ordinary citizens was their excitement about the future of the state and their pride in electing a candidate they'd been told had no chance of winning.

With his bald head, deep voice, and six-foot-four-inch height, Jesse Ventura did not seem to be the kind of person most voters would choose to hold the state's highest office—governor. Rather, he looked like the person he had been before he decided to enter politics: a professional wrestler and action movie hero. But because he wasn't what he called a "career politician," the people had trusted him. As a result, he stood at a podium in the domed Capitol building on January 4, 1999, and took the oath of office.

"We shocked the world," he said in his inauguration speech. "We really did."

Jesse was not the first entertainer or sports figure to have won an election. Former president Ronald Reagan had been a movie actor. Sonny Bono had been a member of the singing duo Sonny and Cher years before he was elected to Congress. Senator Bill Bradley had played professional basketball for the New York Knicks. But Jesse was the only high-ranking American politician who had once been a professional wrestler. Professional wrestling is an outrageous pastime featuring performers as skilled at showmanship as athletics.

Perhaps it could only happen in Minnesota. Jesse often joked that he never worried about his state being taken over by outsiders; you had to be a unique type of person to brave Minnesota's frigid winters year after year. The state has a reputation for being different from the rest. Storyteller Garrison Keillor spins Minnesota-inspired tales of the fictional town of Lake Wobegon on his weekly radio show, and writer Howard Mohr published a book called *How to Talk Minnesotan: A Visitor's Guide.* More importantly, throughout its history, Minnesota has stood apart by electing politicians considered offbeat everywhere else.

The only thing unusual about Jesse's inauguration speech was that it wasn't written down. He talked about the people who were special to him, particularly his parents, both military veterans buried at Fort Snelling National Cemetery. "I can tell right now that the ground's heating up a little bit where they're at," he said, in a voice both amused and sad. "Because I think today, most of all, my mom and dad would look down and say, 'I can't believe it. Look what he's done now.'"

At the governor's side were several men who had served beside him in the Navy SEALs, an elite division of the military devoted to fighting terrorism around the world. Jesse told his audience, "It was a time in my life that created who I am today. . . . I know I can always look back to my Navy SEAL training when the going gets tough, and I know it's not as tough as that."

Sitting in the second row of the audience was actor Arnold Schwarzenegger, who had first appeared with Jesse in the 1987 film *Predator.* The two men had much in common. While Jesse had achieved fame through wrestling, Schwarzenegger first gained his celebrity as a professional bodybuilder. Like wrestlers, most bodybuilders appealed only to fans of their sport. But Schwarzenegger—who became an international superstar—had shown his friend the possibilities of reaching beyond one's limits.

Most of all, the governor was thankful to his family. As he spoke, his fifteen-year-old daughter, Jade, blew him a kiss from her seat. His nineteen-year-old son, Tyrel—six feet, seven inches tall with long side-burns—sat next to her, appearing both amazed by the media attention and overjoyed that his father had done things his own way and succeeded. Their mother, Terry—Jesse's wife of nearly twenty-four years— smiled, tears brimming in her eyes. In the weeks since the election, she'd charmed the people of Minnesota simply by being herself. After the inauguration, when the Venturas were greeting the line of people who had waited outside to meet the new governor, Terry told

Terry shares a proud moment with Jesse as she watches him take the oath of office.

her husband that her feet hurt. Then she kicked off her shoes and continued the conversations in her stockings, acting less like a formal First Lady than like a regular person with aching feet.

In his inauguration speech, Jesse had admitted that his family was "riding along on another one of Dad's escapades, and we're not done yet. And I do owe them a thank you because they're always there for me, no matter what it is I decide I'm going to try next, they're always there with full support. And I just hope that this doesn't change their lives too much, that they can go on being who they are."

To those who remembered Jesse from his days as a wrestler—when he would flex his muscles and call himself the Body—the man who became governor seemed so different from the man they'd booed in the ring. To those listening to him for the first time, he appeared complicated: a tough Navy SEAL who wasn't afraid to show his emotions when he spoke about his family; a man whose speeches condemning "politics as usual" had turned him into the most important politician in Minnesota.

How did Jesse "the Body" become Jesse "the Governor"? To unravel that story, voters, journalists, and politicians looked into Jesse's past and examined the life of the man who "shocked the world."

The kindergartners of Waseca Elementary School in Waseca, Minnesota, show their support.

Chapter **TWO**

THE MAKING OF A LEGEND

JESSE VENTURA WAS ACTUALLY NAMED JAMES GEORGE Janos when he was born on July 15, 1951. His friends and family called him Jim. His father, George, was the grandson of immigrants from Slovakia, in east-central Europe. George had worked as a laborer with the Minneapolis street department. He had grown up in a rough Minneapolis neighborhood called Swede Town, where he was known as one of the boys strong enough to swim against the strong current of the Mississippi River. Jim's mother, Bernice, had come from Iowa. She never forgot the hard times her family suffered during the Great Depression of the 1930s, when many Americans were out of work and struggled just to put food on the table. Because of her family's experience, Bernice vowed to always be able to support herself. As a result, she worked her way through college and became a nurse. George and Bernice met in Minneapolis in 1945, and they married a year later.

Both Bernice and George had served in the United States military during World War II; Bernice was a lieutenant, working as a nurse in North Africa. George fought in Europe, but he kept his war stories to himself. "I never had any idea...that he had seven bronze battle stars," Jim said. "He never spoke of it, and I was his son."

But George did voice strong opinions about politics. He believed that most politicians were "crooked," or dishonest. Sometimes, when he watched President Richard Nixon on television, he would tell his family, "You can see that guy is lying because he's sweating so much."

Jim loved arguing with his father about politics. His older brother, Jan, recalled later, "For Jim, I'm thinking, that's when he first got interested in politics. It must have rubbed off on him."

The Janos family lived in South Minneapolis, a neighborhood in the city where many kids' fathers made a living by working with their hands. Growing up, Jim and Jan played on the sandbars and fished for carp in the Mississippi River, built bonfires on the beach, and sneaked under the fence at the nearby high school to watch football games.

At night, they would listen to professional wrestling matches on the radio. One day at Cooper Elementary School, Jim and his classmates were asked to write an essay about what they wanted to be when they grew up. Jim wrote that he planned to become a professional wrestler.

"The teacher scolded him," recalled his friend Steve Nelson. "[She] said, 'Jim, that's a ridiculous idea. Who would want to be a professional wrestler?'"

As a child, Jim was shy. Because he had never done well in school, he was cautious about raising his hand

It is hard to imagine Jim as a flamboyant professional wrestler by looking at the clean-cut young man in his senior photo.

Jesse shows off his "Best Physique." Classmate Kathy Buck was voted "Best Figure."

during class discussions. But when he entered Sanford Junior High School, others began to notice his athletic skills—particularly on the wrestling mat. His friend Tom Delano remembered that Jim was a "very quick, very focused, very disciplined wrestler, and he knew a lot of the holds."

His athletic success continued at Roosevelt High School. Like his older brother, Jim joined the swim team. The Janos brothers were known as two of the best swimmers at Roosevelt: Jan was team captain in 1966, Jim in 1969. Jim also played on the football team, and during his senior year, he was voted the boy with the "best physique."

Jim's accomplishments in sports increased his self-confidence. No longer quiet, Jim became one of the most popular students at Roosevelt High School—a leader who loved to play practical jokes and make other people laugh. His academic achievements were less admirable, however. "I did enough to get by, and if I liked a class, sometimes I did a little more," he said. "What an opportunity I missed."

When Jim graduated from high school in 1969, he got a job with the state highway department. His brother had joined the military, serving in the Navy SEALs. The SEALs—an abbreviation for *SE*a, *A*ir, and *L*and forces—was a part of the U.S. Navy started in the early 1960s by President John F. Kennedy. The group's aim was to find the best men in the military and send them around the world to fight terrorism. The SEALs specialized in underwater demolition and other difficult tasks. It was said that there was no such thing as a dumb SEAL—if you didn't use your brain, you drowned or were blown up.

When Jan came home to visit after Jim's graduation, he had a long conversation with Jim and his friend Steve Nelson. The Navy SEAL encouraged the young men to go to college and enjoy their youth. But Steve had other thoughts. "I want to join the navy," he told Jim. "I want to do what your brother's doing. And I want you to come with me."

"Are you nuts?" Jim replied. "Didn't you hear what he said? He told us to go to college. He told us to have fun."

But neither of them was sure what they wanted to do with their lives. In the navy, they would learn to handle important responsibilities and travel places they had never imagined.

The two decided to visit a navy recruiting office. Jim recalled, "I said, 'We'll go, we'll listen, that's all. I'm not signing nothing.' We both came out with IDs."

By joining the navy, Jim gave up the chance to attend Northern Illinois University on a swimming scholarship. He later explained, "I was a midwestern boy who wanted to stop communism." At the time, the communist form of government dominated parts of Asia and Eastern Europe. Many Americans feared that communism posed a threat to the United States and democracy around the world.

Jim's parents had mixed feelings about his choice. George was disappointed that Jim was not going to college. But when Jim was told that he might not be allowed to train for the SEALs because the navy thought he was color blind, his mother contacted Minnesota's U.S. Senator Hubert H. Humphrey to ask for help. She knew her son and insisted that the test results were wrong. Humphrey inquired into the matter and determined that Bernice was right. Jim wasn't color-blind and would be allowed to train for the SEALs after all.

THE NAVY SEALS

n 1962, President John F. Kennedy analyzed the wars raging around the world. He concluded that the days of two evenly matched powers doing battle were over. The wars of the future, he believed, would pit a traditional army against a group that was waging "guerrilla warfare"—hiding out in the jungle and staging surprise attacks. To be prepared for this circumstance, Kennedy ordered the creation of the U.S. Navy SEALs.

The term *SEAL* stands for *SEa*, *Air*, and *Land*—the elements these daring commandos have to penetrate. The idea was to establish a group of fighters who would appear out of nowhere, strike their targets, and vanish. Every SEAL mission would be life-threatening. The commandos would be expected to venture up to twenty miles into enemy territory, gather intelligence, ambush the enemy, take prisoners, and cause turmoil in places ruled by America's rivals.

An important tool in these operations was underwater demolition. The SEALs would swim ahead of other military units, setting off explosions and clearing the way for an assault by U.S. forces.

At first, the SEALs simply advised the army of South Vietnam, America's ally in the Vietnam War. But as combat worsened in the Asian nation, the commandos found themselves in actual combat. In Vietnam, the SEALs developed a reputation as courageous and effective fighters against the North Vietnamese army.

After the Vietnam War, the SEAL legacy continued. Navy SEALs played a role in America's invasions of Grenada in 1983 and Panama in 1989, as well as in the Persian Gulf War of 1991. Many military experts consider the SEALs the finest fighting force in the world.

To become a Navy SEAL, recruits have to prove themselves both physically and mentally durable. Navy SEAL training involves surviving in conditions practically identical to battle. It is no exaggeration to say that only the toughest recruits graduate.

Jim traveled to Coronado, California, in September 1969 to begin training. For the first month, recruits went through exercises that challenged their physical strength and skills. The drills became progressively more difficult, leading up to the hardest period—called Hell Week. According to Jim's SEAL commander Larry Bailey, trainees were placed in conditions resembling actual combat: "There are explosives going off around your head, you're denied sleep, and you're denied comfort. You're kept cold and miserable and wet. Hell Week is what traditionally has separated the men from the boys."

Jim had never been tested so hard at anything. But he got stronger with each passing day. At one point, his instructor, Terry Moy, forced him to slog through deep mud. Jim found a dead fish in the muck. He held it up for everyone to see. Moy was annoyed that Jim had stopped for a game of show-and-tell. "So I told him, 'Well, you'd better eat it,'" Moy said. "And he did."

The young man's daring impressed his fellow recruits. But the SEALs who knew Jim's brother were surprised by the differences between the two. Jan was called Clean Janos because he always kept his boots shined and his uniform pressed. Jim was Dirty Janos because he didn't seem to care how he looked.

While Jan kept his thoughts to himself, Jim broadcast his opinions to anyone who would listen. "The first five minutes ... he said more than his brother said in five years," said Garry Bonelli, who served with both Janos brothers. "Jim was up and kept everyone else up. He was going to take on the world."

Commander Bailey also noticed Jim. "My first impression was here's a guy with a little bit of pizzazz," he said. "He was a natural-born leader, had a lot of charisma. He always had a little glimmer in his eye that made you wonder what is he going to do next."

From 1971 to 1973, Jim Janos served in an underwater demolition unit based in the Philippines. He and his friends spent a lot of time meeting girls in the many bars outside the base, but their assignments were full of danger. The platoon was dispatched to various operations around Asia, including Vietnam. Jim survived over one hundred parachute jumps and many other feats. "I dove 212 feet under the water," he said. "I swam in shark-infested waters at night. That's defying death."

In the SEALs, Jim made friendships that would last his entire life. He also started lifting weights, gaining thirty pounds and sculpting the physique that later earned him acclaim as "the Body."

When he returned to the United States, Jim's commanders told him not to reveal any details of his top-secret missions. To this day, he honors that request. "What I did," he says, "is between me and God."

Jesse executes a back-breaking move.

Chapter **THREE**

PROFESSIONAL WRESTLER

AFTER LEAVING THE NAVY IN **1973,** JIM STAYED in California, unsure about what to do next. For a while, he joined a motorcycle club called the Mongols. Some motorcycle clubs are notorious for taking drugs, committing crimes, and beating up rivals. But Jim insisted that he had nothing to do with crime.

"I've never been arrested in my life," he said, "never had cuffs put on me, never been charged with a crime, never spent one day in jail."

In fact, according to Mike Baumgart, a club member Jim knew from the SEALs, Jim left the Mongols because he didn't want to end up dead or in jail.

Returning to Minnesota's Twin Cities of Saint Paul and Minneapolis, Jim enrolled at North Hennepin

Community College, a two-year school. He received high grades in his literature class, where he read and discussed authors like James Joyce and D. H. Lawrence. When he tried out for a play called *The Birds,* he won the role of Hercules, the muscular god from Greek mythology. Anxious to play sports again, he also joined the football team.

But Jim had a difficult time following orders. He particularly objected to the way the coach punished players for small mistakes they made during practice. "I had played the ultimate game—war," Jim said. "In football, they'll penalize you fifteen yards, but you'll still be back to play the next week. In war, the penalty is you die."

After a year, he decided not to go back to school. In 1974, Jim got a job as a bouncer at a bar called the Rusty Nail, in the Minneapolis suburb of Crystal. When customers drank too much and started making trouble, the large Vietnam veteran would approach them and kindly tell them to leave. If they refused, Jim would grab them and throw them into the street.

One night that summer, a pretty, dark-haired girl named Teresa (or Terry) Masters walked into the Rusty Nail. Like Jim, she had grown up in South Minneapolis. She had recently graduated from Saint Louis Park High School and was working as a secretary. Jim said that he fell in love with her immediately. "She walked in and our eyes met, and that was it."

Terry knew there was something special about the big guy who stood in the bar's doorway with his large arms folded. He told her that he had bigger dreams than working at the Rusty Nail, and she believed him. They dated for about a year. Then, on July 18, 1975, when Jim was twenty-four and Terry was nineteen, they were married in a Lutheran ceremony. Afterward, they had a party in a hall above a North Minneapolis bar.

By then, Jim was already planning to become a professional wrestler. His interest in the pastime had been rekindled by his brother Jan, who had attended a wrestling match at an arena called the Minneapolis Auditorium. One of the show's main attractions was an athlete named Superstar Billy Graham. He had bleached blond hair and twenty-two-inch biceps—he called them pythons—bigger arms than many fans had ever seen. In the ring, Superstar flexed his muscles and strutted around in tie-dyed tights and fringed boots. But it was during interviews promoting upcoming matches that Superstar truly "got over"—the term wrestlers use to describe getting the audience excited.

"Look at the biceps, the triceps," Superstar would almost sing, describing his muscles. "I'm the man of the hour, the man with the power. Oooh, baby. Too sweet to be sour." Jan had never seen a wrestler with such a sense of style or such an extraordinary physique. "Wait'll you see this guy Superstar," he told Jim. "He's got the biggest arms on the planet."

PRO-WRESTLING MANEUVERS

n professional wrestling, the action is fast, furious, and full of colorful drama. Here are some of the moves common to the sport.

Atomic Drop A wrestler sweeps his opponent off the ground, then drives a knee into the man's spine as he plummets.

Big Splash A wrestler falls onto a rival, squashing him.

Body Slam A wrestler lifts his foe, twirls him around in the air, and slams him to the ground.

Clothesline A wrestler extends his arm to the side and rushes forward, snaring his rival's neck in his extended arm.

Flying Dropkick A wrestler leaps into the air, kicking his opponent with both feet.

Headlock A wrestler locks his arms around an opponent's head and squeezes.

High Cross Body Block A wrestler flies across the ring, using his body to flatten a foe.

Irish Whip A wrestler slings his rival into the ropes, setting him up for some kind of punishment when he bounces back toward the center of the ring.

Leglock A wrestler wraps his legs around his rival's legs, applying pressure.

Moonsault A wrestler climbs to the top rope and flips backwards onto his opponent.

Neckbreaker A wrestler grips his opponent under the chin and wrenches his neck as the man falls to the mat.

Piledriver A wrestler locks his knees around his opponent's head, holds his feet, and drives his head into the mat.

Powerbomb A wrestler turns his foe upside down and drives his back into the mat.

Powerslam A wrestler clutches his rival, runs across the ring, and slams him onto the canvas.

Suplex A wrestler snaps his foe into the air and holds onto him while falling to the ground.

Jim accompanied Jan to the Minneapolis Auditorium for another wrestling show. They waited through the opening matches until Graham emerged from the dressing room. Professional wrestling has traditionally been an entertainment form similar to comic books or action movies. Good guys (called babyfaces) battle villains (called heels). Superstar Billy Graham was a heel, but everything about him—his looks, his strength, the way he walked—was so sensational that many fans cheered for him.

"Billy Graham walks in with his 22-inch biceps, and the place goes wild," Jim remembered. "I was wearing a T-shirt, okay? And I had a set of arms, too. And the Superstar looked at me, just a glance. But I'm telling you, he looked right at me. Then he started posing."

As fans all around him screamed with excitement, Jim had a thought that changed his life: "I can do this."

He decided to pay a visit to Eddie Sharkey, a legend in the wrestling business because he had trained so many top stars. Fortunately for Jim, Sharkey's gym happened to be in Minneapolis.

For seven months, Jim trained to become a professional wrestler. Because he had no background as a college wrestler, he had to learn a number of amateur moves first. He also had to master the art of "taking bumps"—landing properly when you fall. Most importantly, he studied crowd psychology—how to get the fans to boo, cheer, and get enraged at the right moment.

At the time, wrestlers were very conscious of protecting the business. They were afraid that if fans learned that the matches weren't real life and death struggles, they would stop watching. Before a match even begins, the wrestlers involved know the outcome. They agree on who will be the finisher and the maneuver used to win the match. Other highlights of the clash—when another wrestler jumps into the ring and interferes, for example, or one of the participants uses a folding chair as a weapon, or the referee gets knocked out—are also discussed beforehand. Frequently, the wrestlers understand months ahead of time the many different twists their feud will take. Jim once called the profession a "ballet with violence."

Although the matches are choreographed, the wrestlers often injure themselves by falling on the wrong spot or executing a dangerous move to excite the fans. An estimated eighty-five percent of the injuries that happen on televised wrestling shows are legitimate. Some people say professional wrestling is fake. But Jim asked, "How do you fake a bodyslam? Let me slam you once and you'll see it's not fake."

What's more, wrestlers often go into the ring when their bodies ache, without allowing their wounds to heal. They do it because they don't want to disappoint the fans who paid to see them. "I didn't take professional wrestling as a joke," Jim said. "It's a business, and I learned to perform whether injured or sick."

As he was just starting his wrestling career, Jim had the chance to meet his hero, Superstar Billy Graham, in the gym. Graham described their encounter: "[Jim] just stood back and stared at me for like 30 minutes. He was kind of mesmerized. Then he came over and introduced himself. I liked him immediately. He told me he was going into pro wrestling and mentioned my persona [ring personality] was the reason. My magnetism and the personality I had were really so overpowering to him."

At six feet, four inches tall and 260 pounds, Jim was determined to become as well known as his idol. But he thought he needed a better wrestling name than James Janos. He looked at a map of California, saw the city of Ventura, and decided to make it his last name. He picked Jesse as a first name because he had always liked the way it sounded.

He also determined his gimmick—the role he'd play as a wrestler. Rather than being a rough-and-tumble veteran from the chilly streets of South Minneapolis, Jesse Ventura would be known in the wrestling world as a surfer from San Diego, California. "I was going to be a bleached blond from California," Jesse said, "because everyone hated bleached blonds from California throughout the rest of the country."

Jesse started his wrestling career in Kansas City, Missouri. With $200 in his pocket, he drove from Minneapolis in a beat-up Chevrolet, listening to recordings of Superstar Billy Graham.

After studying all the wrestlers at the Minneapolis Auditorium and listening to Eddie Sharkey's instructions, Jesse knew how to play a perfect heel. He sneered at a crowd in Kansas City to get them to jeer. While fighting against the popular wrestler Omar Atlas, Jesse angered the audience by tossing the babyface over the top rope. The move gave Jesse an automatic disqualification—and a reputation as a sneaky wrestler who refused to follow rules.

Throughout his years as a wrestler, Jesse did everything he could to live up to this image. "Win if you can," he'd boast on television, "lose if you must, but always cheat."

Professional wrestling manager Jimmy "The Mouth of the South" Hart enjoyed Jesse's routine. "He was very articulate and smart," Hart said. "Everything he did was just rambunctious. . . . You can't make a living as a wrestler—talking seven days a week, fifty-two weeks a year—without coming up with things that'll grab the people's attention. Jesse kept the people hanging on every word."

In those days there were dozens of professional wrestling leagues, or promotions, in North America. For example, Florida, Georgia, and Southern California were all separate "territories." Some promotions were based in several states. The World Wrestling Federation (WWF) presented matches throughout the northeastern United States. Wrestlers would drift from territory to territory, staying in one place for a few months, then move on for a fresh start in another part of the country. While some promotions paid well, newcomers often worked in the smaller arenas for low wages. After these wrestlers paid for their motel rooms, meals, and car expenses, they were left with almost nothing. In a two-year period, Jesse put 128,000 miles on his car, driving to different arenas. At one point, he worked for sixty-three days straight.

In 1976, Jesse was working in Oregon. He wore a hooded mask with long blond hair sticking out the back and called himself The Great Ventura. He often

Jesse started out in the wrestling business as the "heel" surfer Jesse Ventura.

hid weapons in his hood to batter the babyfaces. His rivals included Moondog Mayne, Jimmy "Superfly" Snuka, and Dutch Savage. Two times, Jesse won the Pacific Northwest heavyweight championship.

Terry Ventura said that this was the time when her husband learned to perform. Being a heel allowed him "to be more artistic and creative." She recalled how Jesse would stir up spectators by flexing his large muscles and kissing his arms while walking to the ring—"anything to get people riled up, give people something to focus all their frustrations and fears [on]."

Jesse felt that some fans secretly approved of the way he acted. "Some people are smart enough to see that the goody two-shoes are bland, boring people leading boring lives," he said.

Toward the end of his stay in Oregon, Jesse unmasked and actually became a babyface himself. Fans cheered him as he wrestled bad guy Buddy Rose. But Jesse preferred being a heel. When he moved to his next territory, he was again encouraging the fans to hate him.

In the late 1970s, Jesse became one of the best-known wrestlers in the American Wrestling Association, or AWA. This territory was spread throughout the Midwest, and the AWA championship was one of the most important titles in professional wrestling. Since the AWA was based in Minneapolis, Jesse got to act outrageous in front of people who had been his childhood friends and neighbors.

On television, Jesse had a lot of fun making jokes about the Twin Cities, calling them "Turkey Town One and Two." In 1978, while recovering from a knee injury, Jesse took a job as a bodyguard for band members at rock-and-roll concerts that came to the Twin Cities, such as the Grateful Dead, Bob Seger, and Rush. When the Rolling Stones appeared at the Saint Paul Civic Center, the wrestler was asked to introduce the band. Jesse grabbed the microphone and howled in his deep voice, "Good evening, Turkey Town," laughing as the audience jeered.

With Jesse back in Minnesota, he and Terry decided to start a family. Their son, Tyrel, was born in 1979. Even though the AWA was in Minneapolis, Jesse was still away from home for long periods of time. He looked forward to his days off, when he could spend time with his wife and son. Terry said that she and Jesse appreciated the time they had together and made an effort not to waste it by arguing over unimportant issues.

In the AWA, Jesse became an unforgettable performer. Like his hero, Superstar Billy Graham, Jesse wore colorful tie-dyed tights (often without a shirt), along with slit sunglasses, feathered boas, and berets with hanging braids. Because of his muscles, the wrestler called himself Jesse "the Body" Ventura. Like punk rock singers who dyed their hair wild colors, Jesse appeared on television with red, blue, and green streaks in his tresses.

Jesse models one of his many outlandish costumes.

Superstar Billy Graham was impressed by what he saw. "Jesse started out doing the straight Superstar routine, but actually he took my persona farther than I took it. He developed a great interview style, calling himself Jesse the Body, which is a great name. . . . Jesse had the personality to carry it off."

Another wrestler who had patterned himself after Superstar Billy Graham was not as taken with Jesse Ventura. Hulk Hogan developed a rivalry with Jesse both in and out of the ring. The two frequently made critical comments about one another. Part of this was wrestling hype; for much of their careers, Hogan was a babyface and Jesse was a heel. But the negative tone of some of their statements went beyond wrestling. For some reason, their personalities clashed. "Jesse's best move was to cheat and run," Hogan said. "He'd take the tape off his wrists and choke you. He'd gouge you in the eyes. And then, if you cleared your eyes or got the tape off your throat, he'd run for his life."

Other wrestlers described Jesse as courageous. Jesse was once matched against Maurice "Mad Dog" Vachon, a veteran who was considered as tough outside the ring as he was in the arena. Many young wrestlers were careful around Vachon. They didn't want to hit Mad Dog by accident and get him really mad.

But Jesse was different. Mad Dog's niece, Luna Vachon—also a professional wrestler—said, "Frankly, my uncle was one of the meanest, dirtiest sons of guns you ever met. But Jesse smashed him over the head during their match with a steel chair. He didn't lay it in—he wasn't trying to really hurt my uncle— but at least he did it.

"The next day when Jesse came into the dressing room, he was probably thinking he would have to fight for his life. But my uncle went up to Jesse and hugged him. He was proud of this young man for doing what he did. He wanted to put on a good show, and he wasn't afraid of the Mad Dog."

Vachon was just one of many stars Jesse faced in the AWA. In one feud, he was matched against Paul Ellering, who also had a bodybuilder's physique. Jesse called his opponent Eller-rat and got into a weight-lifting contest with him. The contest quickly turned into a fight. Playing the bad guy, Jesse attacked Ellering as he was on the verge of victory, hitting him with the weights.

Eventually, Jesse joined Adrian Adonis to form a tag team. A tag team match usually consists of two wrestlers pitted against another pair. One person from each side starts the match. When the first wrestler wants a break from the action, he tags his partner—hence the name "tag team."

Jesse and Adonis called themselves the East-West Connection because Jesse claimed to be from California, on the West Coast, and his partner said he was from New York, on the East Coast. Of the two, Jesse was more gifted at getting heat—provoking the crowd's fury. Adonis was respected by other wrestlers for being an amazing athlete. Although he struggled with a weight problem, he was fast and agile, able to bounce all over the ring after being struck by an opponent. In July 1980, the East-West Connection won the AWA tag team championship.

"Adrian did the wrestling, Jesse did the talking," observed AWA owner Verne Gagne. "[Jesse] could do Superstar [Graham] better than Superstar."

Jesse was gaining a reputation as one of the best interviews in the wrestling business. Even though the fans booed him in the ring, they found his interview statements amusing. He gave AWA announcer Gene Okerlund the nickname Mean Gene. Before a match against a highly athletic pair known as the High Flyers, Jesse called the duo the High Criers.

Jesse said later, "Wrestling taught me how to ad lib. You had to think on your feet."

Gagne noted, "Jesse realized the value of the interview. He wasn't the greatest wrestler, but he could talk pretty [darn] good."

After losing one tag team championship, Jesse and Adonis "beat up" promoter Wally Karbo on television. As a result, the AWA "suspended" the team, which allowed them to leave the territory. They traveled to the East Coast–based WWF, which would soon become the most powerful promotion in wrestling.

When Antonio Inoki, shown trying to trip his opponent, *was elected a senator in Japan, he proved that a professional wrestler could make it as a politician.*

Chapter FOUR

CELEBRITY

JESSE QUICKLY ESTABLISHED HIMSELF AS A STAR IN
the WWF. Feuding with fellow strongman Tony Atlas
and challenging Bob Backlund for the WWF heavyweight championship brought Jesse a lot of attention
from fans. At a 1982 match in Japan, Jesse fought
Antonio Inoki, one of that country's best-known
wrestlers. Later, the videotape of that match became
a collector's item. Why? Inoki was later elected senator in Japan, while Jesse Ventura went on to become
governor of Minnesota.

In 1983, Jesse returned to the AWA, teaming up with
former Japanese Olympic wrestler Masa Saito. Jesse
called this duo the Far East–West Connection, a twist
on the label he and Adonis had used.

But Jesse had more serious concerns than wrestling. When his daughter, Jade, was born in 1983, she had a rare form of epilepsy. She suffered hundreds of seizures. Doctors were afraid that she would die. But the seizures stopped when they began giving her regular doses of vitamin B_6. Then, when Jade was nine months old, one of her routine shots actually triggered more seizures, and she suffered brain damage. Doctors worried that she might not survive, or that she would not function as well as other kids. But even as a baby, Jade displayed her father's will to defy the odds. With the help of special education classes, Jade grew into a happy, intelligent child.

In the wrestling world, the WWF was expanding. Owner Vince McMahon wanted to end the promotion system that divided North America into small territories. He wanted to rule the entire business himself. To do this, he needed the biggest wrestling names in every region. He approached Jesse and asked if he was interested in leaving the AWA for good. The WWF had weekly programs on cable television, and Jesse was promised that he would be seen in homes from Vermont to Washington State. That would mean bigger paychecks, as well as the possibility of meeting people who could help him in the future. Jesse, who had clashed with AWA owner Verne Gagne over business philosophy, felt that this offer was too good to resist.

He wasn't the only one who had such thoughts. Hulk Hogan also left the AWA. Hogan was crowned WWF champion in January 1984. He soon became a huge star, his fame extending far beyond the wrestling world. People who had never watched a wrestling match knew Hogan's name. There were Hogan dolls and T-shirts and a WWF cartoon show on Saturday mornings. Hogan's fans were called Hulkamaniacs, and the craze he created was termed Hulkamania.

Hollywood stars and rock singers began to hang out at WWF matches, and Jesse Ventura felt right at home

Vince McMahon played Jesse's straight man when they announced matches together.

among them. With his flashy outfits and outrageous statements, he played a big role in what was known as "the rock 'n' wrestling connection."

"A professional wrestler has to expect to be recognized," Jesse told a reporter in 1985. "We're the most recognizable of all athletes. I mean, with a football player, what can you see in that helmet?"

Jesse loved being a celebrity. But he liked being a family man even more. After his out-of-town matches, when the other wrestlers went to nightclubs and bars, Jesse could be spotted sitting alone in a local restaurant, reading a book or newspaper. Then he would return to his hotel, call his wife in Minnesota, and ask about their kids.

Because of his nickname, the Body, Jesse was matched against other muscular wrestlers. He and the Polish Strongman Ivan Putski had an arm-wrestling contest in the center of the ring. Jesse was about to lose when—like a perfect heel—he slugged Putski and smashed him with a chair.

McMahon was slowly building up public interest in Jesse the Body and preparing him for a major feud with Hulk Hogan. This was going to be the highlight of Jesse's wrestling career. But the week he was supposed to challenge Hogan for the championship in Los Angeles in 1985, Jesse developed blood clots in one of his lungs. For several frightening days, he lay helpless in the hospital until doctors were finally able to dissolve the clots.

The incident made him stop and reflect. He had two children and a wife at home. What would they do if Jesse could no longer support them? Professional wrestling could be a lot of fun. And most of the athletes had loyal fans. But Jesse had to think about taking care of his family when his days in the ring were over.

Fortunately, Vince McMahon was well aware of Jesse's talents behind a microphone. He pulled Jesse out of the physically demanding work of wrestling and gave him a job hosting a segment of a WWF television show called *The Body Shop.* During matches, Jesse provided colorful commentary, frequently sitting alongside McMahon and teasing him with hilarious one-liners. To people who were discovering wrestling for the first time, Jesse was one of the wittiest men on television.

"I'm not some big, dumb wrestler," he said. "I know wrestlers who pay more in taxes than most people make. How can they be dumb? Wrestling is ballet with violence. They don't call [male ballet star Rudolf] Nureyev dumb."

Fans who watched WWF shows in the mid-1980s still remember some of Jesse's famous lines. Jesse served as announcer when Uncle Elmer, a bearded, 500-pound wrestler who dressed in worn overalls like a hillbilly, got married on a WWF special on the NBC television network. As Uncle Elmer and his new bride kissed, Jesse told the audience, "They look like two fish going after the same piece of corn." Referring to a brawny wrestler called the Ultimate Warrior, Jesse

Jesse prepares to contribute some "colorful" commentary during a televised wrestling match.

remarked, "He has a million-dollar body and a ten-cent brain." When Randy "Macho Man" Savage cheated during a match with Hogan, Jesse declared, "It ain't cheating unless you get caught."

"Those are your rules, Jess," snapped fellow announcer Gorilla Monsoon.

"No," Jesse responded, "those are American rules, the American way." Even though he was covering a wrestling match, Jesse was making a comment about American society. In politics and business, he suggested, people who cheat are too often rewarded.

Public reaction to Jesse began to change. The more fans heard him speak, the more they liked him. After his lung injury healed, Jesse began wrestling again. But the spectators didn't want to boo him anymore. When his name was announced, cheers rang out through the arena.

Jesse's return to the ring didn't last very long. He was better behind the microphone—and it was far less dangerous. Although he still played the role of heel on the air, spectators shouted "Jesse! Jesse! Jesse!" whenever he sat down at the announcer's table.

On television, Jesse bragged, "I'm tellin' it like it is." Behind the scenes, if he saw something he believed was unfair, he was just as direct. "He is the most honest person I ever met in my life," said his former trainer Eddie Sharkey. "In a business full of shady characters, he always stood out."

He also believed in using his celebrity to pursue other dreams. In 1985, he tried to become a musician, performing concerts that combined the sounds of heavy metal and rap. Two of his songs, "The Body Rules" and "Showdown with Mr. V," were released by a Minneapolis record company. Jesse's image appeared on both sides of the record. In one shot, he is seen in a camouflage outfit, with blood dripping onto his chest from the hole in the center of the record.

Jesse did not mind posing for pictures to sell records. He also found another reason to pose for publicity photos. Although many wrestlers used steroids to pump up their physiques, Jesse was one of the first to admit to it. His wrestling idol, Superstar Billy Graham, had used the drugs and had developed a condition that wore away at his joints. He had to have six hip replacement surgeries. Jesse wanted to persuade other athletes not to make the same mistake. At the height of his wrestling fame, Jesse made several commercials and appeared on posters, urging young people to stay away from the harmful drugs.

In 1986, Jesse tried to start a wrestlers' union. Shortly before "WrestleMania," the WWF's biggest pay-per-view television event, Jesse suggested that the wrestlers refuse to participate until a union was formed. He was told that Hulk Hogan, the biggest name in professional wrestling, would never cooperate. But Jesse felt sure that King Kong Bundy, Hogan's opponent in the main event, would boycott the match.

In the end, Jesse ended up feeling like no one was committed to starting a union as much as he was. He dropped the plan and began to look for opportunities outside of wrestling.

He claims to be the first wrestler to find an agent to negotiate contracts on his behalf. The agent would also try to arrange deals for movies, television shows, and commercials. In 1990, when the WWF didn't approve a video game deal that Jesse's agent had set up, Jesse and the WWF parted ways. He later sued the WWF, claiming the organization owed him royalties—payments related to the sale of wrestling videos. A court awarded Jesse more than eight hundred thousand dollars.

In 1992, Jesse joined the WWF's main rival, World Championship Wrestling (WCW), as an announcer. His contract promised him $950,000 for two years' work. Almost immediately, though, there were problems. Jesse and his bosses had very different views of the wrestling business. Jesse felt he was restricted in what he could say on the air, and he believed that

WCW management would not allow his real personality to come out. Some employees at WCW claimed that Jesse's ego had gotten too big, and that he wanted to promote himself more than the matches. Eventually, WCW allowed Jesse to leave the company. They paid him for the time remaining on his contract, while he stayed home.

Jesse's supporters hailed the outcome as a victory. But Jesse was tired of the wrestling business. He left the industry that had given him his start, ready to conquer other professions.

Jesse Ventura, left, *portrayed Blain, and Bill Duke,* right, *played Mac in the 1987 motion picture* Predator.

Chapter **FIVE**

LIFE BEYOND WRESTLING

THE WORLD OF PROFESSIONAL WRESTLING HAS BEEN described as a sort of fraternity. Wrestlers spend more time with each other than with their own families, traveling and working out together, establishing friendships while they sit in the dressing room waiting to perform. The problem is that many wrestlers never think about what they will do once their days in the ring are over. Some older competitors, feeling lost anywhere but in a wrestling arena, hang around the business until fans are no longer interested in watching them perform.

Even at the height of his wrestling fame, Jesse did not want this to happen to him. He was always on the lookout for other opportunities. Taking advantage of his celebrity, he appeared in his first film, *Predator,* in 1987, alongside his friend Arnold Schwarzenegger, who had become an action movie superstar. Jesse played a U.S. commando searching the jungles of South America for officials who'd been kidnapped by terrorists. But he and his unit soon ended up battling a monster from outer space. As the character Blain, Jesse uttered his best-remembered movie line: "I ain't got time to bleed."

The same year, Jesse and Schwarzenegger teamed up again in *The Running Man,* a futuristic film about a convict whose only chance of freedom is to run for his life away from hunters.

Jesse next appeared in *No Holds Barred,* a 1989 wrestling movie starring Hulk Hogan as a champion facing his toughest challenge. Jesse's on-screen job looked very familiar to most wrestling fans. He played an announcer.

In 1990, Jesse tried comedy, appearing with Linda Blair in *Repossessed.* Blair, who had portrayed a child possessed by the devil in the 1973 classic *The Exorcist,* now played a housewife tormented by the same demon. A year later, Jesse returned to action movies. He appeared in *Ricochet,* a thriller pitting crime master Earl Talbot Blake, played by John Lithgow, against assistant district attorney Nick Styles, portrayed by Denzel Washington.

Abraxas, Guardian of the Universe featured Jesse in his only starring role. In this 1991 movie, Jesse played

Jesse sports a new "do" as Captain Freedom in The Running Man.

Abraxas, an alien police officer sent to Earth to capture his former partner, who left their home planet with evil intentions. One highlight of the film is a conversation Abraxas has with a small boy. After the child tells Abraxas his age, the hero responds, "I'll be 11,862 next Tuesday. That's a little bit more than six, isn't it?"

In 1993, Jesse shared the screen with Hollywood stars Sylvester Stallone, Wesley Snipes, and Sandra Bullock in *Demolition Man,* a crime story set in the future. Jesse acted in two more full-length films, *Major League II* in 1994 and *Batman and Robin* in 1997. In the 1998 short film *20/20 Vision,* he played a marriage counselor who cursed at and smacked patients. He also appeared on numerous television shows, including *The X-Files, Hunter,* and *Outer Space.*

Between his acting jobs, Jesse managed to continue his announcing career. Switching from wrestling to football, he provided commentary for Minnesota Vikings and Tampa Bay Buccaneers games from 1989 to 1991.

But his most challenging job during the years he was appearing in films and working as an announcer grew out of a controversy in the place Jesse had chosen to raise his family. Brooklyn Park, just north of Minneapolis, is the sixth largest city in Minnesota. In 1988, Jesse and his family were living there in a home on the Mississippi River. When Jesse heard about a storm sewer project planned for a nearby wetland, he became outraged, sure the undertaking would endanger the environment. He decided to attend a city council meeting to bring up the issue. Not surprisingly, Jesse voiced his concerns very loudly.

Former Brooklyn Park mayor Jim Krautmeyer said, "There was somebody in the audience talking, and somebody on the sidelines kept speaking out, and I gaveled him quiet. And one of the councilmen whispered to me, 'Do you know who that is?' And I said, 'No, only one person can speak at a time.' And he said, 'That's Jesse Ventura.' And I said, 'Who's that?'"

Jesse said he didn't care whether the mayor recognized his celebrity. He was more interested in being taken seriously as a citizen. Believing that the council was not addressing the wetlands issue properly, he threatened, "You're going to make me run for mayor, aren't you?"

Jesse later joked that there was one big difference between wrestling and politics—politics was dirtier. But Jesse knew how to get the public's attention. In 1990 he announced that he was going to run for mayor, and he campaigned on his Harley Davidson motorcycle. His campaign buttons declared, "Had Enough? Mad Enough? Vote Jesse Ventura." In just a single night, his volunteers blanketed the entire city with flyers.

In most elections, Jesse discovered, the majority of voters stayed home. The secret to victory was to give those people a reason to show up at the polls.

"Brooklyn Park . . . was a city of 56,000 people, and only 2,500 voted in the election before I ran," he said. "The election I ran, 2,500 went up to 20,000."

Krautmeyer had been in office for eighteen years, but Jesse easily defeated him. It was going to be more difficult, however, to run the city. Jesse had told voters that as mayor, he would still have other jobs—like football announcing and acting—and these jobs would take him out of town frequently. But council member Rick Engh, who filled in as acting mayor when Jesse was away, complained, "I probably served more as mayor than he did. He was always away, making movies and everything."

Another former council member, Ron Dow, recalled that Jesse seemed to thrive on confrontation. Once, when Dow and Ventura were arguing, the mayor dared the councilman to step outside. Ventura insists that he wanted to speak to Dow in private, not fight him. But Dow argued, "He likes the conflict. He's said in his interviews, over and over again, about how, if someone wants a good fight, just try him."

Dow said Jesse became angry when council members questioned his policies during meetings. "People on his side got to say whatever they wanted to as long as they wanted to. But when somebody who opposed him got up there, that was a different ball game. He would always find a reason to cut them short."

But Brooklyn Park business owner Dick Gunderson believed that many of those who objected to Jesse's style were angry because he was shaking up the way the city council operated. "He called attention to the problems," Gunderson said, "[and] made us come together and start working on those problems."

During his administration, Jesse helped persuade a firm with eighty-five employees not to leave Brooklyn Park. "It wasn't like I promised them anything," he said. "I just told them how much they meant to our city." Along with several other local politicians, Jesse traveled to Washington, D.C., and convinced the federal government to provide funds for a new highway. He also saw to it that police in his city were given more powerful weapons. Occasionally he rode along with the officers on duty. He claimed that crime and gang activity declined because "we had a mayor with a little bit of military background who knew how to go out and kick some butt. You need to have that little bit of attitude if you're going to deal with crime."

In 1994, Jesse angered some Brooklyn Park city council members when he and his wife purchased a thirty-two-acre ranch in the town of Maple Grove.

He'd already announced that he wasn't running for re-election and wanted a place with a separate apartment for his ailing mother and her medical equipment. There was also enough land for Terry to realize her dream of breeding show horses.

But a few council members protested, saying that the mayor should be removed from office because his new home was outside the city. Jesse argued his case before a judge, claiming that the family spent several nights a week in Brooklyn Park and celebrated birthdays and holidays there. The case was ruled in favor of the mayor.

As mayor of Brooklyn Park, Minnesota, Jesse always spoke his mind at city council meetings. Here, he sits with fellow council members Joe Enge, left, and Craig Rapp, right.

Jesse expressed his opinions on his radio talk show.

With that resolved, Jesse changed careers again. This time, he hosted a call-in talk show on a popular Twin Cities radio station, KSTP-AM. His producer, David Ruth, thought Jesse was perfect for the position. "He'd been outside of wrestling a few years," Ruth said. "He'd made movies. He'd been a mayor, a Navy SEAL. He brought a lot of experience to the table."

Athletes, politicians, authors, and other well-known people joined Jesse in the studio, while listeners called in with their opinions. Jesse enjoyed this forum. He argued with his guests about everything from government to war to sports. He especially liked discussing the 1963 assassination of President John F. Kennedy. The radio host was convinced that Lee Harvey Oswald, the man arrested for the crime, had not acted alone.

Others wanted Kennedy dead and played a role in the murder, Jesse said. Americans wouldn't have justice until Kennedy's "real killers" were identified.

In August 1997, Jesse left KSTP and began hosting a talk show called *Pure Ventura* on a sports-oriented station, KFAN-AM. When Jeff Greenfield, a news analyst for the CNN television network, wrote a novel, he appeared on radio programs around the country. But Jesse's show stood out, in Greenfield's opinion. "By far the most provocative and intriguing and pointed questions were asked by radio talk show host Jesse Ventura," Greenfield said.

Even when the microphone was off, Jesse would keep talking. Newspaper columnist Dan Barreiro, who worked alongside Jesse, recalled, "During commercial breaks, Jesse would leave the studio and continue whatever debate he had begun with the last caller. As he walked around, he would take the debate to whomever he ran into. It could be another talk show host. It could be a producer. It could be an intern. It could be the guy replacing the fluorescent light. . . . Whatever it was, Jesse would get in your face and never let up."

Jesse was so aggressive that at least one coworker decided not to argue with him at all. The man told Barreiro, "I'd just go, 'Absolutely, Jesse. You're right, Jesse. I couldn't agree with you more, Jesse.' It was the only way I could get him to leave me alone so I could go get something to eat."

The Reform party sold these posters to raise campaign money for the party's various candidates.

Chapter **SIX**

RUNNING FOR GOVERNOR

OVER TIME, PEOPLE WHO LISTENED TO JESSE'S radio show began to notice that he mentioned the same subjects over and over. He talked about the Kennedy assassination, and he called for lower taxes. When he discovered that the state of Minnesota had a budget surplus of $4 billion, he was outraged. If there was so much extra money, he asked, why wasn't it returned to the public?

The argument made sense to Jesse's fans. Some began to suggest that he run for governor. What they didn't realize was that Minnesota's Reform party had the very same idea.

The Reform party was started by wealthy businessman H. Ross Perot when he ran for president in 1992.

The Reform movement was supposed to be a third party—an alternative to the Democrats and the Republicans. In Minnesota, where people were used to thinking independently, Perot received twenty-four percent of the vote in the 1992 election—a much larger percentage than in other states.

In 1994, Dean Barkley, a Reform party candidate for the U.S. Senate, drove around Minnesota in a trailer that contained a zoo cage. Inside were models of a donkey and an elephant—the symbols of the Democratic and Republican parties. During the campaign, Barkley was invited to speak on Jesse's radio show. Jesse agreed that a third party was needed to save American politics. He compared the major political parties to two notorious street gangs, the Crips and the Bloods. Jesse called the parties the DemoCrips and ReBloodicans.

After the show, Ventura and Barkley continued their friendship, and Jesse began to embrace the philosophy of the Reform party. "I believe in the Reform party's principles of integrity, dignity, and responsibility," he said, "and [I] desire to be the voice of ordinary citizens who feel they've been shut out of the political process."

Barkley received five percent of the vote in the 1994 election, and he decided to run for senator again in 1996. This time, he asked Jesse to be his honorary campaign chair. The two appeared together at an Independence Day parade in the Minnesota town of Annandale. Barkley recalled, "I noticed that Jesse was receiving most of the cheers from the crowd, even though this was my hometown. I made the comment to Jesse during that parade that [he] should be the candidate, not me. . . . He laughed at me."

Once again, Barkley lost the election. But he and his campaign manager, Doug Friedline, decided that Jesse would make a perfect candidate in the next statewide election. For a period of several months, they called the former Brooklyn Park mayor every two weeks, asking him to run for governor. In September 1997, Barkley and Friedline drove to Jesse's horse farm to discuss the issue in person.

Later, Jesse joked about having that conversation so close to the horses. He thought that horse manure perfectly represented the false promises politicians traditionally made.

Terry Ventura was also included in the discussion. She did not want her husband to run for governor. Jesse explained, "People don't realize the stress of a campaign on the family. And they also don't realize that, when all this is over, it's your family that you have to go back to. So you have to keep this in perspective."

While Barkley and Friedline waited, Jesse and Terry stepped into the barn to talk about the challenge. When they came out, Jesse said that his wife had agreed to allow him to run.

On January 27, 1998, Jesse stood on the icy steps of the State Capitol and announced his decision to run for governor. Although he had never even set foot inside the state offices, he was convinced that he could win. In a letter to his supporters, he explained his logic:

> It's not always true that the candidate with the most money wins. My opponents are boring, and I have a secret weapon the other candidates lack. It's not really a secret. It's an item of public record. But it might as well be a secret to the Democrats, Republicans, press and pollsters who seem to be blind to it.
>
> My secret weapon is the people who will turn out to vote for me who don't normally vote at all. That's exactly how I won my race for mayor of Brooklyn Park (by a landslide!), and that's how I'll win this race for governor.

He promised Minnesota's citizens that he'd be "a truth-telling, non-career politician serving you in the Capitol. Imagine that . . . a governor who cares about people, tells the truth, has no obligation to the big money power brokers, and does not want or need to spend the rest of his life in politics."

Because he had no loyalty to either of the established parties, Jesse was able to pledge to "put people on my team based on their capabilities more than their party affiliation. As a third-party governor, I am more free than any Democrat or Republican to choose the best people for the job. My team would be a team of competent people."

Similarly, he vowed to consider any bill placed before him, regardless of which party supported it. "I can bring the parties together," he said. "I don't care where the bill comes from. It won't matter. If it's good for Minnesota, I'll sign it. . . . As I tell people, there are more Minnesotans than Republicans or Democrats."

Observers who objected to Jesse's candidacy, such as rival Twin Cities radio host Jason Lewis, claimed that Jesse didn't have enough experience to oversee Minnesota's $12 billion state budget. Jesse retorted that "Brooklyn Park didn't go down the toilet" when he was mayor.

Jesse was definitely not a typical political candidate. While most politicians campaigned in suits and ties, Jesse seemed most comfortable in jeans and a Minnesota Timberwolves jacket. At one debate, he appeared in a golf shirt, jacket, and sneakers. He apologized for his appearance, explaining that he had to rush to a high school football game afterward. He had volunteered as a conditioning coach for the Champlin Park High School football team, near Minneapolis.

Young people began to tell Jesse that he was cool. "I thought, 'Well, good enough,'" he said. "'I'll take that.' I am cool. My kids will tell you that I'm a really cool dad. Mentally, I'm still 21 or 22 in a lot of ways."

Even though Jesse was wealthy, drove a fancy car, and owned a ranch, he was seen as an average guy—

Not wearing the customary dress shirt, dress shoes, and tie, Jesse stands out among the participants at a candidates' debate.

someone who jet-skied, listened to rock music, and rented videos with his kids. "I think people are fed up with politics and Jesse is the only authentic working-class candidate," Steve Schier, a political science professor at Carleton College in Northfield, Minnesota, told the *Washington Post* newspaper. "At the same time, politics has become more and more about entertainment. . . . His is essentially a campaign built around a personality and . . . it's working."

What many people found refreshing about Jesse was his willingness to admit that he did not know all the answers. But he said he would work hard to learn how the state government operated and solve problems the best possible way.

Laborer Craig Maiborn told the Minneapolis *Star Tribune* that he was impressed with Jesse. "When I started this job, I didn't know how to do it. But I tried, I worked hard, I learned. Now, it's been four years, and I'm the foreman. So yeah, Jesse can do it. He'll catch on. I did."

Jesse was quick to point out that state laws allowed anyone to run for governor, as long as that person was at least twenty-five years old and a Minnesota resident for one year. "Why can't a wrestler be governor?" he asked. "That's what our country was founded upon."

But getting elected is expensive. A large amount of money is needed to hire a staff, print advertisements, produce television commercials, and travel around the state to make speeches. And Jesse refused to ask for donations. "He felt it was degrading," said Barkley, who chaired Jesse's campaign.

Jesse was also hesitant to accept cash from donors who would then expect favors in return. "With Jesse the Body in office, there will be no big money power brokers behind the scenes, yanking your governor's chain," he told supporters. "I'll be there to serve you, not them."

He further assured his followers that he would not take money from political action committees (PACs), groups willing to contribute to a campaign in order to promote a specific cause. "Campaigns should be based on the issues of the day," he said, "not on who has the most money. . . . I will not accept money from any PACs or special interest groups. My votes will belong to the people, not whoever is paying me to vote for their preference."

Jesse's campaign raised funds by selling T-shirts with the slogan "Retaliate in '98." The shirts were first unveiled at a parade in the town of Delano, Minnesota. "We were swamped with requests to buy them," Barkley said. "This T-shirt became a very successful part of our campaign." Before the election was over, the team sold six thousand shirts at $22 each.

To attract people to rallies, the campaign created a Website. The campaign's media adviser, Bill Hillsman, insisted Jesse's site be as colorful as the candidate. The site was filled with the candidate's dramatic statements, as well as pictures of him. By comparison, Hillsman described opponents' Web pages as dull— a choice "between vanilla and vanilla."

Jesse noted, "The Web is a place you can go without money. Younger voters are very involved in the Web." He pointed to his son as an example, saying Tyrel "knows fifty times more about computers than I do."

The candidate's staff advised him to attend every civic event all over the state, even the smallest ones. Almost all civic groups held forums and debates of some kind. Most of the time, politicians sent representatives to these smaller gatherings rather than going themselves. Since Jesse had a lot to learn about Minnesota's government, he chose to go to as many of the functions as possible. Barkley said the goal was to "get [Jesse's] debating skills sharpened, and to get familiar with the hundreds of issues that were out there—from feedlots to inner city crime."

Wherever Jesse went, he met people who knew him as a wrestler, actor, and radio host. Such status gave him the kind of name recognition few new politicians enjoy. At the Minneapolis Saint Patrick's Day Parade, "he was mobbed and given ovations," Barkley said. "We did not have to ask people to take our literature [the flyers candidates hand out]. They came up to us. . . . We handed out over 10,000 pieces of literature in a parade that went only seven blocks. . . . This was the first time I began seeing the 'Jesse Phenomenon' and his ability to instantly connect with people."

Although Jesse hadn't watched wrestling in years, he visited a WCW television taping at the Target Center in Minneapolis. "We obtained second-row seats," Barkley recalled, "gave out Jesse signs and literature before the event, and made a planned late entrance. . . . Jesse brought the house down. When he entered the building unannounced, the entire crowd began chanting, 'Jesse, Jesse, Jesse'. . . . There was a constant stream of people coming up to Jesse for autographs, and to give Jesse encouragement to run for governor."

At the Minnesota State Fair in late August 1998, Jesse created even more excitement. As Jesse talked to the people, crowds began to form around his booth. Thousands of T-shirts were sold, and twenty thousand Minnesotans signed up to help with the campaign. Supporters began calling themselves the Bod Squad.

One of the most critical choices he had to make was choosing a running mate. If Jesse won the election, his running mate would become lieutenant governor—and would be in the position to take over the state if Jesse died or resigned. He approached Kent Hrbek, the retired star of the Minnesota Twins, but the baseball player declined.

"I thought it was great," Hrbek said. "But I'm not a politician. Then again, neither is Jesse."

Jesse's advisers told him that Minnesotans were most concerned about taxes—a subject frequently mentioned on his radio show—and education. The advisers also took a survey and found that men were four times as likely as women to support him. "Jesse had a real gender problem," Barkley said. "We needed a female educator to balance the ticket."

Mae Schunk had been an award-winning teacher and school administrator for thirty-six years. A member of the Ventura campaign team recommended her as a candidate for lieutenant governor. Like Jesse, Mae had strong opinions and would be seen as a practical and down-to-earth person. When she and Jesse met, they instantly connected.

"I am a product of the Minneapolis public schools, and I am a supporter of the public schools," Jesse explained when he introduced Schunk as his running mate. "But I do not pretend to have the answers to all the questions in schools today. So I have turned to an expert, to a dedicated teacher who knows how to in-

Former teacher Mae Schunk promised to focus her efforts on education as lieutenant governor.

spire students, who uses creativity and enthusiasm to encourage children to learn."

Schunk advocated smaller class sizes, and she wanted students to study the basics: history, geography, English, math, and science. She also had high standards for teachers, insisting that each should have to pass a competency test before being permitted to step into the classroom.

With Schunk helping to shape his education policies, Jesse announced that he wanted all public schools to have computers and Internet access for students. He also called for classes for parents to keep up with what their children were studying.

Jesse was outspoken about many other issues as well. He told voters that taxpayer money should not be used to build a new baseball stadium for the Minnesota Twins baseball team. "When owners and players are making millions, the stadium should and can be built with private money." Handguns should be available to law-abiding citizens who have proper training, Jesse argued. He said that politicians should serve no more than two four-year terms in office, and he vowed to leave the governor's mansion after eight years. On the issue of taxes, he pledged, "I will veto [reject] any new taxes, and any increase in existing taxes. And I keep my word."

Although he was popular with young people, Jesse told them some things they didn't want to hear. While he supported scholarships for poor students with high grades, he made it clear that he did not believe the government should pay for the average student's college education. "If you're smart enough to go to college," he told a group of high school students, "you're smart enough to figure out how to get there." For those who couldn't afford college, Jesse suggested they follow his example: join the military and then go to school with funds provided to veterans.

One of Jesse's most controversial ideas involved prostitution. He said he would consider legalizing it, as had been done in the Netherlands and in parts of Nevada. "People are going to do stupid things," he said, referring to those who spend money on prostitutes. "We cannot sit and every time someone does something stupid, make it a law and have the government come in, because if you do that, you're going to lose your freedoms."

When asked about his position on granting certain rights to homosexuals, Jesse did not hesitate. He had gay friends, he said, and he believed that they had the right to marry one another. "I have two friends who have been together forty-one years," he said. "If one of them becomes sick, the other one is not even allowed to be at the bedside. I don't believe government should be so hostile, so mean spirited. . . . Love is bigger than government."

His position on drugs also caused controversy. He agreed with a group that had studied drug-dealing gangs. They had determined that making drugs legal would lessen the gangs' power. Jesse also supported the right of a doctor to give marijuana to a patient in severe pain. "Studies and individuals have indicated that medical use of marijuana can significantly aid sufferers of glaucoma [an eye disease], chronic pain and the pain associated with terminal cancer," Jesse stated. "We should not withhold this treatment option from so many people who could benefit from it."

Early in the campaign, Jesse championed his positions on his radio show. When people said it wasn't fair for him to have so much free air time, Jesse responded, "I could alienate voters as much as get them, couldn't I? People could listen to me on the air and say, 'I would never vote for that guy.'" Jesse even urged his station to give his opponents free air time. "I'd love to see these other candidates spend three hours answering questions from the public like I do

A RENEGADE TRADITION

Minnesota has lived by a renegade political spirit since it became a state in 1858. Jesse Ventura is one of a long line of unconventional candidates who have inspired the people of Minnesota.

- Farmer-Labor party candidate **Floyd B. Olson** was elected governor of Minnesota in 1930. The Farmer-Labor movement represented angry farmers and low-paid workers who felt that the government ignored their needs. Throughout the 1930s, the Farmer-Labor party was the most powerful in the state, trailed by the Republicans and Democrats.

Using the plain language Minnesotans liked, Olson said he hoped the government would go "straight to hell" if it could not provide jobs and food for the people. Olson had a great deal of charisma, but he also had a reputation for gambling and womanizing. Among his friends were criminals, Communists, and people with questionable pasts.

Still, Olson knew that Minnesotans appreciated his honesty and down-to-earth way of talking. When asked about his reputation, he told the truth rather than double-talking. "That's a cross I got to bear, boys," he joked to reporters. "Pray for me."

- In 1938, Minnesota Republican **Harold Stassen** became the youngest governor in United States history at age thirty-one. (Bill Clinton later came close to breaking Stassen's record, taking the oath of office as governor of Arkansas at age thirty-two.) Stassen played by his own rules, making political appointments without the approval of his party. He was appointed by Democratic president Franklin D. Roosevelt to represent the United States in creating the United Nations at the end of World War II. Stassen also ran for president ten times, but never received the Republican nomination. The last time he attempted to win America's highest office was 1992, when the "Boy Governor" was eighty-five years old.

Governor Karl Rolvaag, far right, *tours a Minnesota artificial limb factory in 1969.*

- In 1945, **Hubert H. Humphrey**—the father of Jesse's Democratic opponent Skip Humphrey—was elected mayor of Minneapolis, the largest city in Minnesota. Humphrey received national attention when he made an unforgettable speech at the 1948 Democratic National Convention, demanding that the party embrace the civil rights movement. Some white Democrats from southern states—where blacks and whites were forced to live, work, and go to school separately—were so outraged that they walked out of the convention.

- When Democrat **Karl Rolvaag** defeated Republican governor Elmer Andersen by only ninety-one votes, Andersen would not accept the result. He refused to leave the governor's office, forcing Rolvaag to work in the Capitol basement. Finally, a court ruled that the election was valid. Andersen considered the ruling for several days, then decided to leave the office. Rolvaag's inauguration was organized almost overnight. He took the oath of office nearly three months late.

- In 1981, **Rudy Perpich,** a dentist and son of a Croatian miner, began a ten-year stretch as governor of Minnesota. He promoted education and wanted to expand opportunities for women and minorities. By the time he left office, Minnesota was the only state in the nation with more women than men on its Supreme Court. But Perpich was also labeled "Governor Goofy" by *Newsweek* magazine for his many quirks. He demanded, for example, to have two portraits of himself in the state Capitol—one for each full term he served as governor.

  After Perpich left the governor's mansion, he moved away from Minnesota to start a political career in his father's home country. But in Croatia, he failed to repeat the success he had enjoyed in the American Midwest.

on a daily basis," he told listeners, "see if they can handle it."

In the summer of 1998, KFAN decided that Jesse should leave his show, at least until the campaign was over. His advisers were relieved. "This freed Jesse to start campaigning full time, except for football practice," Barkley said. "Up 'til then, he had to be in the Twin Cities from 10:00 A.M. to 1:00 P.M. every Monday through Friday. The event was a major turning point in the campaign, for the positive. Jesse could now appear on all the competing radio stations that up until then were reluctant to have him on."

But even those closest to Jesse weren't sure he could defeat his opponents. After the primary election in September, the field had narrowed to two candidates from the Democratic and Republican parties. Democrat Hubert Humphrey III, known as Skip, was the son of former vice president Hubert H. Humphrey. From the time Skip was a boy, he'd been raised to lead. He had been Minnesota's attorney general—the lawyer representing the state—for sixteen years. In this role, Humphrey had sued the tobacco industry for costs associated with smoking-related illnesses among the state's citizens. Because of his efforts, the state was awarded a $6.1 billion settlement. Minnesota's top unions and lawyers were backing Humphrey.

Republican Norm Coleman had the support of many of the state's business leaders. He'd been an assistant attorney general for sixteen years and was serving as the mayor of Minnesota's capital, Saint Paul. When asked about the Reform party candidate, Coleman called the Ventura campaign "irrelevant" and said a vote for Jesse would be a "wasted" one.

Naturally, Jesse had plenty of comebacks. He portrayed his opponents as politicians who had been living off taxpayer money for years. "I think people are hearing something new, something different," he said of his campaign. "They know I'm going to be straight with them. . . . How many jobs have I had since I graduated from high school, while both my opponents, all they've done is collect government checks."

Jesse also insisted that the other candidates would never have been able to endure the demands of being a Navy SEAL, as he had. "This is nothing compared to Navy SEAL training," he said of the campaign. "Norm Coleman and Skip Humphrey would wet their pants. They'd be crying for their mommies after the first day."

Most observers agreed that Jesse was the funniest man in the race. But they weren't sure if that would translate into success. "I think we're going to win," Jesse assured them. "The public wants someone to look up to." He paused before delivering his punch line. "I'm six-foot-four. They're not."

Jesse lets out a victory cry as he is crowded by his supporters at Ventura campaign headquarters.

Chapter **SEVEN**

VICTORY

TWO MONTHS BEFORE ELECTION DAY, MOST OPINION polls predicted that Democrat Skip Humphrey would win the 1998 Minnesota governor's race. Humphrey considered Republican Norm Coleman a serious opponent. But he didn't seem to be taking Jesse seriously.

As the Democratic and Republican candidates planned a series of debates, Humphrey made an unusual request to include Jesse. Political insiders immediately recognized the strategy. As the front runner, Humphrey thought that a third candidate would provide a distraction from Coleman's attacks on Humphrey's positions. And the former wrestler might even lure a few voters away from the Republican candidate, helping Humphrey score a larger victory.

Jesse promised to keep the debates dignified. When asked to name his opponents' worst ideas, he replied, "This seems like an open invitation to negative campaigning. . . . I'm not running against any one candidate. I'm running against the two-party system."

Some of Jesse's fans from his wrestling days were hoping to see a trace of the bad guy who went on television each week and promised to pulverize his

A WAR BETWEEN POLITICAL SONS

Even before the national media discovered the "Jesse phenomenon," the press was already following the 1998 Minnesota governor's race. That's because the Democratic primary featured some of Minnesota's most famous families. Four prominent Minnesotans were vying to represent the Democratic party on the ballot in the November election.

Candidate Ted Mondale, a lawyer and former state senator, was the son of Walter Mondale, a former vice president, United States senator, and ambassador to Japan. Candidate Mike Freeman was the son of Minnesota's twenty-ninth governor, Orville Freeman. Another candidate, Mark Dayton, was part of the family that owns the Dayton Hudson department store corporation, which includes the Target store chain.

The eventual winner of the Democratic race was Hubert Humphrey III, also known as Skip Humphrey. Humphrey was the son of former vice president Hubert Humphrey, the most respected Minnesota politician of the twentieth century.

opponents. But Jesse insisted that his goal was to discuss the issues that were important to Minnesotans.

Jesse's critics predicted that he would be lost in the debates. They knew he was likable and well spoken. But next to Humphrey and Coleman—whose lives had been devoted to politics—the Reform party candidate was expected to look like an amateur.

That illusion was shattered from the very first debate, held on October 1, 1998. Jesse's diligence in attending so many small meetings across the state had paid off. He understood the concerns of Minnesotans from every region of the state. While Humphrey and Coleman mainly concentrated on finding fault in each other, Jesse stated his opinions loudly, in language people could understand. By the second debate, both of his opponents admitted that Jesse seemed to have some worthwhile ideas.

A forum on October 6 in Hibbing, Minnesota—the heart of the state's Iron Range—showcased the best of Jesse. The Range has a long, colorful history of iron mining, and many residents still work in the taconite (low-grade iron ore) mines. These people tend to be suspicious of professional politicians who appear removed from the common person. In 1984, when civil rights leader Jesse Jackson was running for president, he received an incredibly warm reception on the Iron Range. It wasn't because Jackson was African-American (most of the residents of the region are white), but because he related to the struggles of working

Americans. Jesse, with his background as a Vietnam veteran, professional wrestler, and action movie actor, was able to touch the same nerve.

"There's certain things that set me apart from the other two candidates," Jesse said at the beginning of the Hibbing debate.

> I am the only governor candidate who won't be held by strings when he goes over to that office, and won't have to do "payback time," as I said in the movie *Predator* a few years ago. . . . I am the only candidate that truly served his country in the military. Neither of the other two candidates saw fit to do that in their youth. . . . I am not here to make a career out of politics. This is not my career. I'm here answering a call that I think Minnesota needs answered because, if you look nationally, look at what the Democrats and Republicans have done. . . . If this isn't the time for a third party, then when?

When someone at the forum asked Jesse about his role models, he became choked up and had to turn around for a moment to compose himself.

> My mentors are my mom and dad. My father had an eighth-grade education. My mom was a nurse in North Africa, and they taught me what it was like to serve your country. Because it's those

people who give us our freedoms today, not the politicians. It's the men and women that have to go fight the wars because of what? Failed political policy from the career politicians. So my mom and dad stand head and shoulders in guiding me to everything I've done today.

Someone else asked Jesse how tax dollars from area mines should be distributed. "Oooh, that's a toughie," he responded. "I would have to back off on that, and say I need to study it a lot more because I'm very honest, and if I don't know the answer, I'm not going to sit here and try to B.S. the people."

This was the type of question Jesse's opponents hoped would convince Minnesota's voters that he didn't have the necessary experience to hold the state's highest office. But Jesse's response had the opposite effect. Nobody knows all the answers, viewers concluded, and it was nice to finally hear a candidate admit it.

At the end of the debate, each candidate was asked to make a closing statement. When it was Jesse's turn, he ran his hands across the lectern and said, "Nothing here on the podium. I don't have professional speechwriters. I don't come here with notes. I don't have professional handlers. That's the difference between me and the professional career politicians. . . . A vote for Jesse Ventura is just that. It is a vote for Jesse Ventura and no one else."

As the audience applauded, Jesse continued, "You've heard a lot of talk up here tonight about jobs, jobs, jobs from both sides. . . . I know what it's like to lose a job. I know what it's like to go out and compete to . . . get a job."

As the speech progressed, Jesse's voice got louder and louder. This was the Jesse who was a master of the wrestling interview, the man who could persuade fans that the upcoming match would be more spectacular than anything they had ever seen. Pointing at the audience, he boomed, "So I want you to think very hard November third, and I want you to be the Minnesotans that set the stage and send the message. . . . 'I'm embarrassed by the Democrats and Republicans in Washington.'. . . Elect Jesse Ventura as the governor, and it will ring across America. Trust me. And it will send a message to them to put the people before the parties."

The ovation that rose from the crowd followed Jesse for the rest of the campaign. After each debate, the percentage of voters committed to him increased. Chris Gilbert, a political science professor at Gustavus Adolphus College in Saint Peter, Minnesota, noted that Jesse used the forums to single out his opponents and say, "'Look at them bickering. This is what my campaign is a rejection of.' When they attacked each other, his stock rose," said Gilbert.

Jesse also clowned around to get the voters to laugh with him. During one debate, he was asked how he

Students all over Minnesota supported Jesse's campaign.

would deal with members of the state legislature who disagreed with his positions. Going back to his wrestling persona, the Body flexed his muscles.

Steve Schier, chair of the political science department at Carleton College, observed that Jesse is "charismatic. He's warm. He's colorful. Coleman and Humphrey were much more conventional politicians, and provided a nice gray backdrop. Every act needs a straight man, and he had two of them."

Because Jesse was running on the Reform party ticket, his name was linked with Perot, the party's founder who had run for president in 1992 and 1996. Perot was a powerful, nationally known figure, and his presence in Jesse's campaign would have been helpful. But as Jesse toured Minnesota, talking to potential voters, he felt that he was on his own.

His advisers contacted the Reform party's main office in Dallas, Texas. They asked for a contribution to the Ventura campaign, or at least help in persuading a bank to provide a loan. But campaign chair Dean Barkley complained that the organization did "little of anything to help the campaign." As a result, Jesse distanced himself from Perot and his movement.

In the end, Jesse didn't need Perot—or anyone else—to campaign for him. The former wrestler and actor was enough of a celebrity to draw a crowd. His campaign manager, Doug Friedline, noted that young people were attracted to the candidate "in part because of his wrestling persona. They all grew up watching him on TV."

Matt Crouch, a senior at Saint Cloud State University, echoed the same feelings. While watching Jesse speak at his school, the student said, "Hey, he's a hero to us—the wrestler, the guy he played in *Predator.*"

Jesse knew that many young people did not take advantage of their right to vote, and he went out of his way to get them excited about his campaign and the election. He visited colleges and spoke at lively rallies. "Humphrey reached out, too, but to parents," said University of Minnesota student Andy Ditter. "That's why almost everyone I know is voting for Jesse."

Joe Johnson, a freshman at Augsburg College in Minneapolis, commented, "My parents are voting for Coleman. But Jesse's the one who came here to speak."

Jesse amused people of all ages with his campaign song, a spoof of the "Theme from *Shaft.*" *Shaft* was a 1971 movie about a hip private eye in New York's tough inner city. In the campaign song, Jesse stepped into Shaft's role. "When the other guys were cashing government checks," the tune went, "he was in the navy, getting dirty and wet."

Some noted that Jesse's style was more fitting for a rock star than a politician. And he never hesitated to remind voters that he was a huge fan of rock music. In one radio ad, he said, "This is Jesse Ventura, and this is what I stand for. . . . I believe Led Zeppelin and the Rolling Stones are two of the greatest rock bands."

As election day drew near, the Ventura campaign hired Bill Hillsman, a political advertising expert whose offbeat ads helped college professor Paul Wellstone become a U.S. senator from Minnesota in 1990. "He's so refreshing," Hillsman said of Jesse. "Jesse's worked in movies. He's been a pro wrestler. He understands pop culture. He gets it. He knows what's going to play in public, and he's not afraid to take chances."

Hillsman started working on radio, television, and newspaper advertisements, even though campaign staff hadn't found a bank willing to give them a loan to pay for the ads. But Jesse's advisers believed the commercials were essential because he was still in last place in the polls. On September 23, 1998, a survey found that, if the election were held that day, Jesse would receive just ten percent of the vote—as opposed to forty-nine percent for Humphrey and twenty-nine percent for Coleman.

With the help of Minneapolis City Council member Steve Minn, the campaign found a bank willing to do business with Jesse. "This was the toughest problem we had to face in the campaign," Barkley said, "and was the absolute key for us having a legitimate chance to compete." The Ventura organization spent nearly $100,000 on the campaign, compared to over $2 million for Humphrey and over $3 million for Coleman.

Hillsman came up with the idea of a television commercial featuring a Jesse Ventura action figure. When he told the candidate about the concept, Jesse was thrilled. "We're doing that," he immediately stated. "What else have you got?" The advertising executive was amazed at how quickly Jesse responded. "It was the fastest decision I've ever seen a politician make," Hillsman said. "No seventeen layers of handlers telling him, 'It's too risky. . . .' Just *boom*, go do it."

Jesse broke new ground in political advertising with this action figure commercial. The doll on the left is the "evil Special Interest Man."

The ad appeared on television in October. It showed children playing with action figures—one of Jesse, the other an evil Special Interest Man. Special Interest Man wanted to give Jesse money in exchange for his political support. But the Jesse doll snapped, "I don't want your stupid money." After the commercial ran, the Ventura campaign began receiving about ten thousand dollars a day in donations.

Jesse was no longer being dismissed as a hopeless third-party candidate. His numbers were rising in the polls, and people began to think he actually might have a chance of winning. Mark Kaplan, a Minneapolis investment banker, wrote in the *Star Tribune,*

> The Ventura momentum really began when the polls showed that he was earning fourteen percent of the vote or more, enough to be taken seriously. During the ensuing weeks, thousands of conversations occurred among office people riding together in elevators, people waiting in food lines, morning and evening joggers, parents watching their children's athletic events, workers sorting mail. Citizens discovered that their friends and coworkers were also considering voting for Ventura. . . . People convinced each other to vote for Ventura and, in doing so, they also convinced themselves.

Shortly before the election, Jesse was feeling confident. "We're going to win it in two weeks," he declared, "and they're not going to know what hit 'em." But he was not about to sit back and wait. At the end of the campaign, he led a caravan of twenty vehicles, touring the state for seventy-two hours in a motor home. During the trip, his campaign ran a commercial in which Jesse pretended to be the famous sculpture *The Thinker* by Auguste Rodin. Wearing only a pair of shorts, Jesse sat on a pedestal, resting his chin on his fist, pondering the problems ahead of him. An announcer listed his qualifications and finally urged viewers to vote not for Jesse the Body, but for Jesse the Mind. Jesse then looked up at the camera, smiled, and winked.

"We needed a closing ad that would show the voters the warm, real family man Jesse was," Barkley explained. "We had to reach the women voters who had not yet warmed up to Jesse."

No one was sure if the strategy would work. Two days before the election, Jesse was still running last, with a projected twenty-seven percent of the vote, compared to thirty-five percent for Humphrey and thirty percent for Coleman. But support was still building. And some Democrats and Republicans were starting to change their minds.

On Election Day, it became clear that Minnesotans felt very strongly about the election. Sixty-one percent of all registered voters came to the polls—the highest turnout in the nation. In some communities, there were lines of people in the street waiting to vote.

Something that helped Jesse was a Minnesota law

that allows people to register to vote on Election Day. Thousands of college students decided to take this opportunity. Almost all these new voters picked the former wrestler. Many of Jesse's supporters said they hadn't voted in years, or had never voted. Surveys showed that about one out of every eight people who showed up at the polls said they would have stayed home if the election had been between Humphrey and Coleman. Some people claimed that they didn't make their choice until they stepped into the voting booth.

"People tell me they had a hard time with this decision," said Mark Sump, a political analyst. "Skip was not that different from Coleman. Jesse was very different. Jesse had no government experience. [Some people thought] 'He's a pro wrestler. We'll be a

Many voters were surprised by the long lines at some of Minnesota's polling places.

laughingstock. What am I gonna do?' But Skip wasn't giving people reasons to vote for him. And so it was a complicated decision. . . . In the end, Jesse created a feeling of emotion that the others didn't."

Steve Frank, who coordinated a poll for Saint Cloud State University, observed, "Jesse's like [former president] Ronald Reagan. Strictly speaking, people didn't agree with [Reagan] on a lot of important issues. But they liked and trusted him. He was like their dad. This was a personality election."

Kenneth Nuckols, resident of a Minneapolis suburb called Eden Prairie, explained his decision to vote for Jesse in a letter to the *Star Tribune:* "For most of this decade, America has been searching for something different, something refreshing. . . . It all has to do with honesty and trustworthiness. Those are qualities we have ceased to find in our political leaders. . . . The political system in this country is broken. Thank you, Jesse Ventura, for having the courage to run."

At his home on Election Day, Jesse tried to relax. He watched the movie *JFK,* about one of his favorite topics, the assassination of John F. Kennedy. Then the Ventura family listened to news reports from the polling places. "The only way we could tell we might win was from word on the street," says Jesse's son, Tyrel. "What we heard from the street was everyone was voting for him."

About a thousand of Jesse's followers gathered at Canterbury Park, a racetrack in the town of Shakopee, to watch the election results on television. When the voting booths closed at 8:00 P.M., early reports indicated that Jesse was doing better than expected. His supporters went wild, chanting, "Landslide! Landslide! Landslide!"

In the lead, Jesse entered the room and stood at the podium. As his fans cheered, Jesse urged them not to get too excited. After all, only thirty percent of the vote had been counted.

"The night is young," he said. "We're only one-third around the racetrack. The important thing to remember is that at least at one time, we led this race."

His supporters thought Jesse was being too cautious. The other candidates were on the ropes, and the crowd expected nothing less than a knockout.

"It's all yours!" shouted one man.

"Bring it home, Jesse!" someone else yelled.

As the night went on and more results poured in, it was clear that Jesse's lead was not going to disappear. "It was closing in on midnight," Jesse recalled later. "And all of a sudden . . . the television camera showed my name with that check by it." On election night, charts listing the various candidates appear on television, with check marks next to the winners' names.

When the final numbers were tallied, Humphrey—the man everyone thought would run away with the race—was in last place, with twenty-eight percent of the vote. Coleman had thirty-four percent. And Jesse the Body Ventura, the former professional wrestler who had once called the Twin Cities Turkey Town One and Two, was the most popular person in Minnesota. Jesse won the election with thirty-seven percent of the vote. The governor-elect ranked highest among every age group under sixty.

"It's overwhelming," Jesse boomed to his cheering supporters. "We shocked the world. Nobody thought we had a chance." He said he knew that voters picked him because they felt they could trust him, and he vowed not to disappoint them. "During the campaign, I didn't make a lot of promises because I'm a person who believes that he doesn't make promises that he can't keep. But I'm going to make you one simple promise tonight. I promise you I will do the best job that I can do. . . . I will probably make mistakes. But remember we all make 'em. And if they're mistakes from the heart, then you don't have to apologize for them."

Of Jesse's two opponents, Coleman had been the most critical of the Ventura campaign, warning that a vote for Jesse would be wasted. Now it was Jesse's turn. "Let them say, 'A vote for Jesse is a wasted vote,'" the governor-elect proclaimed. "I'll say, 'We wasted them with wasted votes.'" He also recalled that Coleman had called the Ventura campaign "irrelevant." "Well," Jesse gloated, "irrelevancy won."

Coleman, who would continue his job as mayor of Saint Paul, was willing to take back his words. "There was a spark out there that he ignited, and you have to give him credit for that," the Republican said of the new governor.

Humphrey compared himself to Iraqi dictator Saddam Hussein, whose country was attacked by U.S.–led forces during the 1991 Persian Gulf War. "Now I know what Saddam Hussein felt like when those bombs started falling."

Television and radio stations around the United States interrupted their local election coverage to bring the stunning news from Minnesota. "The people of Washington could not be more surprised if [Cuban leader and U.S. enemy] Fidel Castro came loping across the midwestern prairie on the back of a hippopotamus," commented CBS news anchor Dan Rather.

After leaving the podium at Canterbury Park, Jesse spotted a bouquet of roses sent to him by a supporter. "Did I die?" he joked.

As Jesse and his wife celebrated with a bottle of champagne in their hotel room that night, they kept reliving the events of the last several months. "We couldn't sleep," said Terry Ventura. "We kept looking at each other, saying, 'Hey, you're the governor!' 'Hey, you're the First Lady!' It's unbelievable."

The next morning, Jesse was handed a copy of the Minneapolis *Star Tribune*. On page one, in large black letters, the headline screamed, "Ventura Wins." Across the river, the *Saint Paul Pioneer Press* newspaper gave him a new name: "Jesse the Gov." The governor-elect could hardly believe what he was reading. Finally, his campaign manager Doug Friedline told him, "Jess, I guess we didn't dream last night."

Jesse shocked the world enough to make the cover of a special Midwest edition of Time magazine.

Chapter **EIGHT**

ROCKING ON

THE REACTION TO JESSE'S VICTORY WAS IMMEDIATE.
Reporters from all over the world rushed to
Minnesota to interview him. *Time* magazine printed a
special issue for Minnesota, with a smiling Jesse on
the cover. The governor-elect was named one of *People*
magazine's twenty-five most intriguing personalities of
the year. A Jesse Ventura action figure—similar to the
one in his campaign ad—appeared in stores. President
Bill Clinton seemed amused by the news of the former
wrestler's election, telling reporters, "I think you're
going to have a lot of politicians spending time in
gyms now."

Jesse also found the attention comical, joking to his
fellow Minnesotans, "Heck, maybe we should move

the [U.S.] Capitol here." He boasted that his presence in the governor's mansion would boost state tourism.

Nineteen-year-old Tyrel Ventura seemed to have the same sense of humor as his father. "I suppose I'll be a little bit more popular," he said after the election. "And I'll probably get a few more dates."

A few days after the election, Jesse went to Fort Snelling National Cemetery to spend some time visiting the graves of his parents. He wondered how they would have reacted to the news that their youngest son had become governor of Minnesota.

Jesse was aware that his family was about to go on a journey much different from anything they had experienced in the past. "I'm going to somehow try to continue [normal] life," he said. He paused and added, "It will never be the same."

Every member of the family now went about their daily chores accompanied by bodyguards. "I guess they need them," Jesse said. "But I used to be the one providing the security, not needing it. A guy my size goes wherever he wants."

Terry Ventura wasn't immediately comfortable with her new role as Minnesota's First Lady. In fact, she spent the first three days after the election in tears. "I never felt so alone in a sea of people, and so inadequate," she said. "I always felt I could handle anything, but this just seemed like such a big job."

Jesse worried about his wife. "But then, I knew her too," he said, "and I know the kind of strength she has."

Before long, Terry was focusing on the issues she found important. As a mother, she cared about children, especially special education students such as her daughter, Jade. Terry's experience as a horse breeder also made her sensitive to the needs of farmers. The governor-elect took his wife's opinions seriously and said he planned to listen to her advice on agriculture.

Before winning the governor's race, Jesse had made a number of bold statements. Now he was forced to live up to his pledges. He promised to return the surplus money in Minnesota's budget to citizens, but he admitted it would take some time to work out the details. He did, however, reconsider his idea of sliding down a rope from the dome of the State Capitol. "I'll do some fun things, but I don't want to cheapen the office," he explained.

Like many from Minnesota, Jesse had been looking forward to attending a Rolling Stones concert in Minneapolis about a month after the inauguration in 1999. But when he was offered a private seat, the governor declined. Throughout the campaign, he'd told supporters that he would not accept these types of favors. He was going to keep his word.

All types of strange requests came into Jesse's office. An inmate serving time at a prison in the nearby town of Stillwater volunteered to take over the state's prisons. Another Minnesotan applied to be the governor's official hot air balloonist. One citizen told Jesse during a radio call-in show that she hoped he would spend time having fun in the yard of the governor's mansion. A college student called to schedule a private meeting with the governor.

At a national training session for new governors, held shortly after the election, Jesse attracted the greatest amount of attention. Delaware Governor Thomas Carper said that he was interested in meeting Jesse because of his wrestling background.

"I want to learn the sleeper hold," Carper said. "That might help with my two boys. And all of us would like to learn the half nelson for dealing with the legislature."

Jesse didn't mind the remarks. He also appreciated the bumper stickers that started showing up on the state's cars, which bragged, "Our Governor Can Beat Up Your Governor." Jesse proclaimed that he was the toughest politician in the country. "I think I can go on the record and say if you were to lock any governor in the cage with me, we know Minnesota's governor will win."

Despite such playful statements, Jesse took a thoughtful approach to the challenges ahead. Since he had never been inside the state legislative offices, he had much to learn. Before his inauguration, Jesse took what some called a crash course in government. He traveled from one state agency to another, meeting with workers and finding out from them how the government operated.

"I learned that there were buildings that the governor hadn't set foot in for thirty years or more," he

The governor-elect was greeted by costumed employees when he toured some of Minnesota's state offices.

said. "That baffled me a little, but it fit right in with my campaign of doing things a little bit differently."

But, no matter what department he visited, Jesse found himself cheered by workers who were happy to see a governor standing in their office and asking about their jobs. "You're only as good as the people you surround yourself with," he said. "In order for me to be successful, I need all the people that work in state government to have pride in their jobs, and do their jobs to the best of their ability. And if they do that, we will be successful."

As an independent governor (the only other governor in the U.S. who was not a Democrat or Republican was Angus King of Maine), Jesse did not have to appoint Democrats or Republicans to important positions in his administration just because of party loyalty. One day, Jesse was talking with his chief aide, Steven Bosacker, about the people who might be hired to work for the governor. Bosacker asked Jesse, "When you look around the table at your cabinet, what do you want to see?" Jesse had a one-word answer: "Competence."

Although Jesse had often clashed with the city council in Brooklyn Park, he hoped to have a better relationship with the state legislature. "I'm not here to fight anyone," he said. "This is about compromise. I can do that. This is serious work. We all work for the people. They voted for me, and I can do it."

To those who were nervous about Jesse's explosive style, the governor's words were reassuring. "I simply will say I will do the best job I am capable of doing," he said. "I'm not a rebel. I'm not coming on board to create some sort of rebellion."

Attitudes like that made some people wonder whether Jesse was preparing himself for higher office. "Jesse has been talking about being president of the United States for many, many years," said WWF owner Vince McMahon. "He is convinced he will be president, and maybe he will."

But Jesse insisted that he was not thinking about the presidency. Governing Minnesota would be difficult enough. The only reason he entered the governor's race, he said, was because he believed the people deserved a different kind of leadership. "I didn't need this job," he said. "I ran for governor to find out if the American dream still exists in anyone's heart but mine. I'm happy to report it does."

On January 16, 1999, 14,000 fellow believers joined the new governor at the Target Center in Minneapolis for a party that Jesse called the People's Celebration. The event was the highlight of two weeks of festivities surrounding the inauguration. During that time, Jesse had returned to Brooklyn Park to release an eagle in the wetland that had originally inspired him to enter politics, back when he ran for mayor. He also had a

Jesse came back as "the Body" to celebrate with his fans and campaign supporters at the People's Celebration.

Minnesota's first family: from left to right, *Jade, Jesse, Terry,* and *Tyrel.*

potluck dinner with a group of farmers and coffee with workers at a Ford auto plant.

At the People's Celebration, members of motorcycle clubs mingled with conservatively dressed suburban mothers; men with gray hair and large bellies; ladies in evening gowns; and teens with pierced ears, noses, and eyebrows. A man who was wearing a dress told reporters that he came because Jesse believed in including everybody.

The unusual crowd was entertained by the University of Minnesota marching band and the cheerleaders for the Minnesota Vikings football team. Crunch, the mascot of the Minnesota Timberwolves basketball team, rappelled from the rafters. Blues-rock singer Jonny Lang—a teenage Minnesota local—had both Jesse and Terry Ventura dancing and fifteen-year-old Jade jumping out of her seat. The rock group America sang their classic song "Ventura Highway" in the governor's honor. Then British rocker Warren Zevon changed the words from his song, "Send lawyers, guns, and money" to "Send, lawyers, guns, and Jesse" as the crowd howled.

Zevon invited Jesse on stage to sing a special version of the hit song "Werewolves of London."

"For one night," Jesse declared, "the Body's back. The Body's back."

"Who put a flying headscissors on Hubert Humphrey?" Zevon sang.

"Jesse the Body," Jesse roared. "Werewolf of Minnesota."

Gone was the dark blue suit Jesse had worn at his inauguration. Instead, he sported sunglasses, a beige scarf wrapped around his head, a purple feather boa over a fringed leather jacket, a T-shirt showing rock legend Jimi Hendrix, a hoop in one ear, and a serpent and skull in the other.

Observers assumed that the night was Jesse's last chance to get his wild ways out of his system. But, after less than a year in office, he surprised them. In July, 1999, Jesse announced that he would perform as a referee at a WWF pay-per-view event called SummerSlam. Ventura's opponents claimed that it was not dignified to participate in a wrestling match. But Jesse replied that there was nothing wrong with a governor who wanted to have fun.

As he said at his inauguration party, "If this is any indication of what the next four years will be like, we're going to have a hell of a good time. Rock on!"

SOURCES

14   Jesse Ventura, interview by Tom Snyder, *The Late Late Show with Tom Snyder*, CBS, November 17, 1998.

14   Pat Doyle and Mike Kaszuba, "Rebellious Road," Minneapolis *Star Tribune*, January 10, 1999.

15   "Jesse Ventura," *A&E Biography*, December 30, 1998.

16   Ibid.

17   Tom Meersman and Anne O'Connor, "Ventura Spends Day with Vets, Students," Minneapolis *Star Tribune*, January 12, 1998.

17–18   Jesse Ventura, interview by Brian Lamb, "Minnesota Governor Elect Profile," *American Profile with Jesse Ventura*, C-Span, December 15, 1998.

18   Keith Elliot Greenberg, "Jesse Ventura Takes the Rock 'n' Roll Challenge," *Faces Magazine*, June 1985.

20   "Jesse Ventura," *A&E Biography*.

20   "Eating His Own Words," Combined News Dispatches, *Newsday*, January 2, 1999.

20–21   Doyle and Kaszuba, "Rebellious Road."

21   "Jesse Ventura," *A&E Biography*.

21   Jesse Ventura, interview by Jay Leno, *Tonight Show with Jay Leno*, NBC, November 17, 1998.

21   Greenberg, "Rock 'n' Roll Challenge."

23   *The Ventura Files*, "The Quote Machine," n.d., <http://www.venturafiles.com/default.asp?section= QUOTE> n.d.

24   Greenberg, "Rock 'n' Roll Challenge."

24   Jesse Ventura, *The Late Late Show with Tom Snyder*.

25, 27   Mark Kriegel, "Wrestler-Governor, He Bodyslammed Pols," *New York Daily News*, November 8, 1998.

28   Jeffrey Zaslow, "Govern or Get Out of the Way," *USA Weekend*, January 8–10, 1999.

28   Keith J. Kelly, "Ventura Inks $500K Book Deal to Pen Bio," *New York Post*, December 14, 1998.

28   Julie Cart, "Pro Wrestling Governor Out to Show He's No Joke," *Los Angeles Times*, November 5, 1998.

29   Mark Kriegel, "A Prayer for Billy Graham," *New York Daily News*, November 29, 1998.

29   Ibid.

30   Kriegel, "Wrestler-Governor."

30   Jesse Ventura, interview by the author, January 1998.

32   Bob von Sternberg, "Ventura Is Master of Reinvention," Minneapolis *Star Tribune*, November 4, 1998.

32   Greenberg, "Rock 'n' Roll Challenge."

34   Kriegel, "A Prayer for Billy Graham."
34–35   Paul Gray, "Bodyslam," *Time*, November 16, 1998.
35   Jesse Ventura, interview by the author.
36   Kriegel, "Wrestler-Governor."
36   Ibid.
37   Ibid.
42   Greenberg, "Rock 'n' Roll Challenge."
43   Matt Bai and David Brauer, "Jesse Ventura's Body Politics,"
      Newsweek, November 16, 1998.
43–44   "Jesse 'The Body' Ventura Quotable Quotes," n.d.
      <http://wwfiswar.simplenet.com> n.d.
45   "Wrestling Up Support," Minneapolis *Star Tribune*, November
      5, 1998.
52   John Rabe, "Ventura's Mayoral Record, Indicator of
      Gubernatorial Term?" Minnesota Public Radio, November 11,
      1998.
53   Jesse Ventura, *Tonight Show with Jay Leno*.
53   Ibid.
53   Rabe, "Ventura's Mayoral Record."
54   Ibid.
54   Ibid.
54   Gray, "Body Slam."
54   John Jeter, "The Body Slams into Politics," *Washington Post*,
      October 22, 1998.
56   Jesse Ventura, interview by the author.
57   Eric Black, "Victory Makes Ventura the Story," Minneapolis
      Star Tribune, November 5, 1998.
57   Dan Barreiro, "Jesse Era Like Jesse Will Be Loud,"
      Minneapolis *Star Tribune*, November 6, 1998.
60   "E-Debate 98," *Minnesota e-democracy website*, n.d.
      <http://www.e-democracy.org/mn-forum/
      e-debate98w/rb6ventura.html> n.d.
60–61   Dane Smith, "Diary of an Upset," Minneapolis *Star Tribune*,
      November 8, 1998.
61   Jesse Ventura, *The Late Late Show with Tom Snyder*.
62   Jesse Ventura, "Jesse's Message to His Supporters and Friends
      about Funding His Campaign and Winning the Election,"
      Official Cite of the Jesse Ventura Volunteer Committee, n.d.,
      <http://www.jesseventura.org/campaign98/jvsuprt.htm> n.d.
62–63   "E-Debate 98," *Minnesota e-democracy website*, n.d.
      <http://www.e-democracy.org/mn-forum/
      e-debate98w/r6ventura.html> n.d.
63   Bai and Brauer, "Jesse Ventura's Body Politics."
63   Jim Ragsdale, "Debate Puts Ventura Under Bright Lights,"
      Saint Paul Pioneer Press, October 27, 1998.
63   Bai and Brauer, "Jesse Ventura's Body Politics."
64   Jeter, "The Body Slams into Politics."

65 Rosalind Bentley and Susan Hogan, "Ventura Gets Votes from All Walks of Life," Minneapolis *Star Tribune*, November 5, 1998.

65 Jesse Ventura, interview by the author.

65 Dane Smith, "Diary of an Upset," Minneapolis *Star Tribune*, November 8, 1998.

65 Jesse Ventura, "Jesse's Message to His Supporters."

65–66 Ibid.

66 Smith, "Diary of an Upset."

66 Tom Hamburger, "Ventura Campaign Tactics Captivate Washington Crowd," Minneapolis *Star Tribune*, December 2, 1998.

66 Jeffrey Zaslow, "Govern or Get Out of the Way," *USA Weekend*, January 8-10, 1999.

66–67 Smith, "Diary of an Upset."

67 Ibid.

67 Ibid.

68 Jim Souhan, "Jesse-Herbie Ticket Almost Was Reality," Minneapolis *Star Tribune*, November 5, 1998.

68 Smith, "Diary of an Upset."

68–69 Jesse Ventura, "Jesse Chooses Award-Winning Elementary Teacher as Running Mate," *Official Cite of the Jesse Ventura Volunteer Committee*, June 30, 1998, <http://www.jesseventura.org/ campaign98/newsre07.htm> n.d.

69–70 Ibid.

70 Ibid.

70 Meersman and O'Connor, "Ventura Spends Day with Vets, Students."

70 Gray, "Body Slam."

71 Jeter, "The Body Slams into Politics."

71 Jesse Ventura, "Medical Use of Marijuana," *Official Site of the Jesse Ventura Volunteer Committee*, n.d., <http://www.jesseventura.org/campaign98/issues/iscrime.htm> n.d.

71 Laura McCallum, "Jesse Ventura: Reform Party Gubernatorial Candidate," *Minnesota Public Radio News*, July 6, 1998, <http://news.mpr.org/features/ 199807/08_mccalluml_ventura/index.shtml> n.d.

72 Dan Hoffenning, "It's an Uphill Battle for Any Third Party to Endure," Minneapolis *Star Tribune*, November 11, 1998.

72 Tom Hamburger and Patricia Lopez Baden, "Minnesota's Past Is Prologue," Minneapolis *Star Tribune*, November 29, 1998.

74 Ibid.

74 Smith, "Diary of an Upset."

75 Jeter, "The Body Slams into Politics."

75 Dennis Cass, "The Running Man" *ABCNews.com*, October 27, 1998, <http://more.abcnews.go.com/ sections/us/DailyNews/pn_jesse981027.html> n.d.

75   Jeter, "The Body Slams into Politics."
78   "E-Debate 98," *Minnesota E-democracy Website,* n.d.
      <http://www.e-democracy.org/mn-forum/
      e-debate98w/r6ventura.html> n.d.
82   Cart, "Pro Wrestling Governor Out to Show He's No Joke."
83   Gray, "Body Slam."
83   Smith, "Diary of an Upset."
84   Bob von Sternberg, "As Ventura Motors Along, He Hits with
      Young Voters," Minneapolis *Star Tribune,* November 2, 1998.
84   Ibid.
84   Paul Levy, "Young Voters Go Down Ventura Highway,"
      Minneapolis *Star Tribune,* November 4, 1998.
84   Ibid.
85   Patricia Lopez Baden, "This Candidate Knew How to Market
      Himself," Minneapolis *Star Tribune,* November 5, 1998.
85–86 Smith, "Diary of an Upset."
86   Baden, "This Candidate Knew How to Market Himself."
87   Mark Kaplan, "Pure Democracy," Minneapolis *Star Tribune,*
      November 8, 1998.
87–88 Rochelle Olson, "Wrestler Barges into Minnesota Race,"
      Associated Press, November 20, 1998.
88   Smith, "Diary of an Upset."
89–90 David Peterson, "There Were Signs but Switch to Ventura
      Surprised Pollsters," Minneapolis *Star Tribune,* November 6,
      1998.
90   Ibid.
90   "Race Came Down to Honesty, Trustworthiness," Minneapolis
      Star Tribune, November 7, 1998.
90   Pat Doyle, "Supporters Cheered Loudly and Proudly,"
      Minneapolis *Star Tribune,* November 4, 1998.
91   "Ventura Stages Shocker in Minnesota," *Associated Press,*
      November 4, 1998.
92   Ibid.
93   *The Ventura Files,* "The Quote Machine."
93   Ibid.
93   Bob von Sternberg and Pat Doyle, "In Victory, There Is No
      Rest for the Weary Body," Minneapolis *Star Tribune,*
      November 5, 1998.
93   Ibid.
95   *The Ventura Files,* "The Quote Machine."
95–96 Ibid.
96   Ibid.
96   von Sternberg and Doyle, "In Victory, There Is No Rest for the
      Weary Body."
96   Bai and Brauer, "Jesse Ventura's Body Politics."
96   Jesse Ventura, *Dateline,* NBC, December 22, 1998.
96   Ibid.
97   Bai and Brauer, "Jesse Ventura's Body Politics."

98   Tom Hamburger, "24 Hours and 36 New Friends for Ventura,"
       Minneapolis *Star Tribune*, November 14, 1998.
98   Jesse Ventura, *Tonight Show with Jay Leno.*
98–99 Jesse Ventura, interview by the author.
99   Jesse Ventura, speech observed by author, 1998.
100   Jesse Ventura, interview by the author.
100   Cart, "Pro Wrestling Governor."
100   Dane Smith and Robert Whereatt, "New Day, New Challenge,"
       Minneapolis *Star Tribune*, November 5, 1998.
100   Vince McMahon, interview by Matt Lauer, *Today*, NBC,
       November 5, 1998.
101   Kelly, "Ventura Inks $500K Book Deal to Pen Bio."

SELECTED BIBLIOGRAPHY

Bai, Matt, and David Brauer. "Jesse Ventura's Body Politics."
Newsweek, November 16, 1998.

Gray, Paul. "Bodyslam." *Time*, November 16, 1998.

Greenberg, Keith Elliot. "Jesse Ventura Takes the Rock 'n' Roll
Challenge." *Faces Magazine*, June 1985.

Kriegel, Mark. "Wrestler-Governor, He Bodyslammed Pols."
New York Daily News, November 8, 1998.

Ventura, Jesse. Interview by Brian Lamb. "Minnesota Governor
Elect Profile." *American Profile with Jesse Ventura*." C-Span,
December 15, 1998.

Zaslow, Jeffrey. "Govern or Get Out of the Way." *USA Weekend*,
January 8–10, 1999.

Minneapolis *Star Tribune* coverage of Jesse Ventura's election
campaign and first months in office (11/2/98–1/12/99).
Staff writers: Patricia Lopez Baden, Dan Barreiro, Rosalind
Bentley, Eric Black, Pat Doyle, Tom Hamburger, Dan
Hoffenning, Susan Hogan, Mark Kaplan, Mike Kaszuba,
David Peterson, Dane Smith, Neal St. Anthony, Bob von
Sternberg, Robert Whereatt.

INDEX

OTHER TITLES FROM LERNER AND A&E®:

ABOUT THE AUTHOR

Keith Elliot Greenberg is a journalist, television producer, and author of more than a dozen books for Lerner Publications. He's been field editor of the *World Wrestling Federation Magazine* since 1985 and assisted Jesse Ventura with his monthly column for that publication. More recently, he covered the Ventura election and inauguration. A lifetime New Yorker, Keith lives in Brooklyn with his wife, Jennifer, and son, Dylan.

AUTHOR ACKNOWLEDGMENTS

The author wishes to thank the following people for assisting him in crafting this book: Jim Byrne, Alan Sharp, Susan Slabicki, Vince Russo, Ed Ricciuti, Theresa Coffino, Dave Meltzer, Danny Lerner, Lee Engfer, Michele Moore, Kirsten Frickle, Mike Zipko, Cody Shimek, Mark Mostad, Mike Hopkins, and Jennifer and Dylan Greenberg.

PHOTO ACKNOWLEDGMENTS

© Craig Skinner/Globe Photos, Inc., 2; © Andy King/Sygma, 6; Reuters/Eric Miller/Archive Photos, 10, 102; AP/Wide World Photos, 12, 38, 41, 56, 58, 64, 89, 94; Seth Poppel Yearbook Archives, 15, 16; © Titan Sports/Sygma, 15, 22, 34; North Hennepin Community College, 31; © John Barrett/Globe Photos, Inc., 44; Hollywood Book and Poster, 48, 51; Star Tribune/Minneapolis-St. Paul, 55; Minnesota Historical Society, 73; Reuters/Scott Cohen/Archive Photos, 83; © 1998, North Woods Advertising, Minneapolis, MN, 86; © Bruce Kluckhohn, 99; © Andy King, 101; Photo courtesy of the author, 112.

Cover photos
Hardcover: State of Minnesota—Office of the Governor-Elect, front; © Titan Sports/ Sygma, back.
Softcover: Reuters/Eric Miller/Archive Photos, front; Reuters/Scott Cohen/ Archive Photos, back.